IMAGES
of America

SOMERS

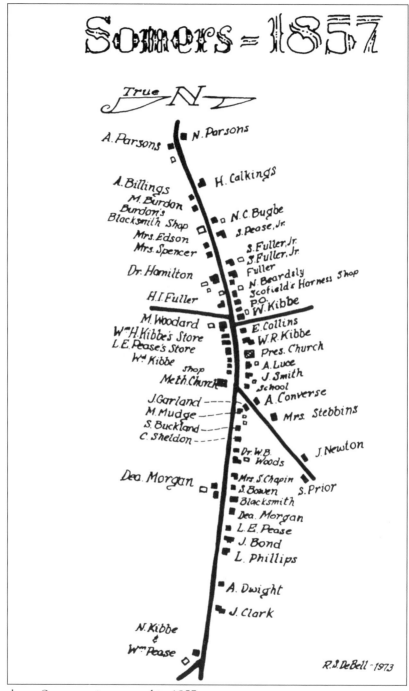

This map shows Somers as it appeared in 1857.

On the cover: Erskine Martin drives Henry Root Kibbe's horses at the barns of the Piedmont estate, located at 235 Main Street.

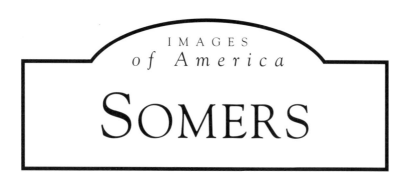

IMAGES
of America

SOMERS

Somers Historical Society
Jeanne Kenyon DeBell

Jeanne K. DeBell

ARCADIA

Copyright © 2001 by Somers Historical Society.
ISBN 0-7385-0489-0

First printed in 2001.

Published by Arcadia Publishing,
an imprint of Tempus Publishing, Inc.
2A Cumberland Street
Charleston, SC 29401

Printed in Great Britain.

Library of Congress Catalog Card Number: 00-110236

For all general information contact Arcadia Publishing at:
Telephone 843-853-2070
Fax 843-853-0044
E-Mail sales@arcadiapublishing.com

For customer service and orders:
Toll-Free 1-888-313-2665

Visit us on the internet at http://www.arcadiapublishing.com

*This book is dedicated to the memory of Robert Percoski, selectman
from 1990 to 1996. His was the first official voice
advocating the relocation of the Somers Free Public
Library to its lovely and useful new site.*

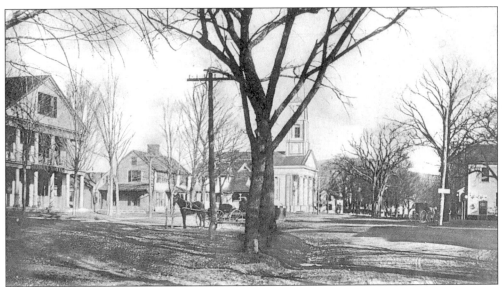

The Congregational church dominated the heart of the village, as can be seen in this 1885
view. The hotel, or Somers Inn (left), served as the stagecoach stop. In the center is a horse
trough, partially hidden by the trees.

CONTENTS

ACKNOWLEDGMENTS

Images offered in this book have come both from the photographic archives of the Somers Historical Society and from the attics and albums of generous donors. The project has been well publicized, and the impetus to donate has increased with the realization of the historical value of gathering pictorial records before they vanish in the mists of time. In a sense, then, this is the work of the entire Somers community.

The images have been arranged by a dedicated committee; Jeanne Kenyon DeBell and Phyllis and Ralph Lumb met at least twice a week for many months and bore the main burden of assembling materials. Phyllis Lumb meticulously researched genealogical and land-record sources, assembling a body of data that enriches the society's library. Long-term residents Whitlock Davis, Leone Lakonski, and Katherine Welch served as consultants and experienced enough to separate the inevitable fictions from the facts of which they had personal knowledge. Richard DeBell contributed photographs from 1982 to date and edited the captions for this book. Steven Lumb has put his computer expertise to advantage, scanning all the early drafts to keep the committee on track. We are indebted, too, to Allison Brooks Collins, trained as an architectural conservator, who gave us a heightened perception of the uniqueness of the Somers Historical Museum and wrote the introduction to this book.

Reference is occasionally made to the Howes Brothers—Walter, George, and Alvah, traveling professional photographers during the period from 1882 to 1907. They took thousands of glass plate photographs of families, homes, and businesses throughout southern New England. The Ashfield Historical Society in Massachusetts now cares for this historical collection.

Many of the images in chapter 4 were provided by the Connecticut Historical Commission in Hartford, Connecticut.

INTRODUCTION

Have you ever fantasized about transcending time and space and arriving upon the threshold of yesterday to explore firsthand its mystery, its enduring allure? Perhaps you have even contemplated constructing a device for that purpose in your garage—a time machine, some massive black box to serve as a portal to the past. But did you ever pause to realize that such a contraption already exists? Conceived in the 1830s, the camera is the time machine you are seeking. However, this black box cannot transport the entire human body, but only a portion of it, something infinitely more critical—the human mind. You are holding in your hands the fruits of the camera's labors, but moreover the essence of a small New England town known as Somers. Steeped in agricultural tradition and natural majesty, Somers is nestled between Soapstone and Bald Mountains on the northern border of Connecticut, where it plays host to languidly meandering miles of the Scantic River and the blazing autumnal acres of the Shenipsit State Forest. The Massachusetts town of East Longmeadow forms its northern boundary, while Connecticut's Stafford, Ellington, and Enfield encompass Somers to the east, south, and west. This book therefore serves as a treasure map to Somers and the wondrous secrets buried there, sparkling beneath the surface of the present.

The first settler of the town during its formative years was Benjamin Jones, originating from the town of Enfield and arriving in Somers territory c. 1706. He erected a small house, slightly to the northeast of the present hardware store on Main Street. At first, the Jones family used the premises as a summer farm, hunting lodge, and emergency refuge "from the Indians." The threat of attack then seemed imminent. A formalized settlement did not emerge until 1713, with the arrival of Timothy Root, Edward Kibbe, James Pease, and John McGregory. These founding members of a community were soon accompanied by such names as Horton, Wood, Collins, Cittron, Davis, Sexton, Parsons, Blood, Purchase, Rockwell, Felt, and Fisk. Soon thereafter, the first church was erected in Somers in 1727. Congregational in denomination, its raising signified a joyous celebration for the 180 residents of the precinct, who would no longer have to journey to Enfield for services.

As the American Revolution marched into the New World, a small but valiant company represented Somers, a community vigorously supporting autonomy from England. By this time, Somers had acquired a more civilized appearance and a more expansive area of settlement, with houses speckling the lowlands and the bases of Bald, Perkins, and Rattlesnake Mountains. Also notable was the appearance of Somersville, known as Billings Mills in reference to the family that operated the sawmill and later the gristmill and satinet mill on the south side of the millpond. The mills of this vicinity would later boast the sought-after kersey wool of the

Somersville Manufacturing Company, a nationally recognized textiles firm founded by Rockwell Keeney in 1879 and perpetuating until 1969.

Aside from the American and Industrial Revolutions, Somers also played an active role in the transportation revolution, beginning in 1783 with Post Road pioneer Capt. Levi Pease, who founded the first stagecoach route from Boston to Hartford. Pease later expanded his stage operations from Portsmouth to Savannah and served as the first U.S. mail carrier for all of New England. Today, at the juncture of Routes 83 and 190, the Somers Inn (built in 1804 or earlier as the Kibbe Hotel and later known as the Olde Homestead Inn) bears testimony to the prominence Somers once possessed as a rest stop for weary Post Road wayfarers. By the early 1900s however, Somers had left the stage in the dust, as high school students boarded trolleys bound for classes in neighboring Enfield. The town's central intersection now echoed not with clattering wagon wheels, but with revving engines at the midtown auto showroom.

Somewhere between the coach and the combustion engine, Somers prospered as a source of agricultural products. From creamery milk to orchard cider, from champion racing stock to veritable groves of tobacco, Somers cultivated a land-linked wealth that fueled its more industrialized neighbors. Interspersed among harvest schedules and farmlands were lessons and one-room schoolhouses as well as such prestigious educational institutions as a women's preparatory or "select school." Located at the Claudius Pease House on 611 Main Street (currently Colonial Flower Shop), the school was founded in the mid-19th century by Mary Chapin Pease, a Somers native and the second principal of Mount Holyoke Seminary, the first American women's college. However, Pease was not alone in her quest to enhance educational opportunities in Somers, for in 1896 Laurinda Collins Whitney, another former Somers teacher, funded the construction of the town's first free public library. Since relocated to a new site, this animated, art glass–studded structure now houses the Somers Historical Society Museum. Therein lie countless other tales of Somers heritage too numerous to recount here, but readily accessible to all with a desire for discovery.

Today, the citizens relish Somers as one of the few surviving small towns in America. In fact, Jeanne Kenyon DeBell, author of this work, has ransacked museum archives, heirloom albums, and private photograph collections to compile this graphic tribute to the town's kaleidoscopic past. Quite adept at such research, DeBell is a 38-year veteran of the Somers Historical Society. Since its inception in 1962, this organization has reaped her talents as a general member, longtime curator, and multiple-term president. Fellow past and present society members, Ralph and Phyllis Lumb, Whitlock Davis, Katherine Welch, and Leone Lakonski have also furnished personal anecdotes, photographic identifications, historical trivia, and general consultation services to enrich this volume. Once a meager 25-pound purchase, Somers has evolved into an invaluable open-air archive.

This priceless repository of material culture, architectural heritage, and human legacy is emblazoned upon our pastoral landscape and immortalized in the pages of this book by the time machine we call photography. Turn the page! Time travel awaits.

—Allison Brooks Collins

One

SOMERS CENTER

After King Philip's War, the area of north central Connecticut was rapidly settled, with growth radiating from a number of small nuclei. The development of Somers is owed to the position of Somers astride the road to anywhere and everywhere. Somers coalesced around Billings Mills (Somersville), Kibbe's Mill (North Somers), Woodville (Turnpike Road), and, as the seat of local government, Somers Street (Somers Center).

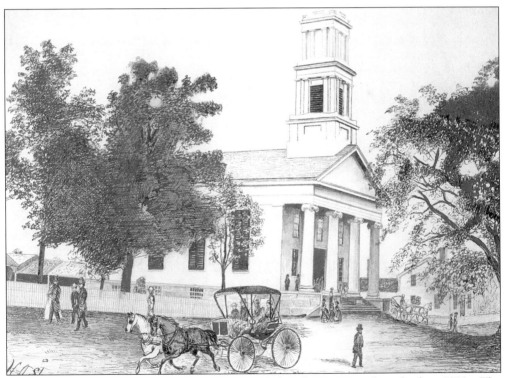

This pen-and-ink drawing of the Congregational church was created in the late 1800s. The artist, Henry J. Shaw, was related to Laurinda Collins Whitney, the donor of the Collins Library. (Loan, Somers Congregational Church.)

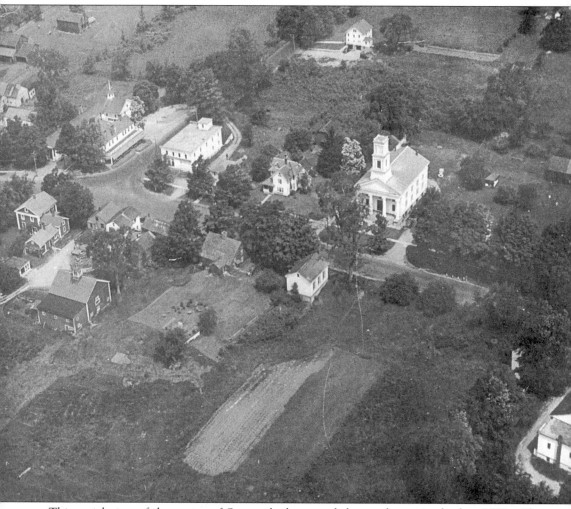

This aerial view of the center of Somers looks toward the northwest in the late 1930s. The Congregational church faces Guild Hall across Somers Street (Main Street), at right center. At upper left center, the Somers Inn and the big, square "Potato Warehouse" (since razed) flank Springfield Road. The warehouse, with big plate-glass windows, was built as an automobile dealership. Opposite the inn is the Woodward House, which still stands on the east side of South Road (Route 83), although the structures to its right have fallen victim to fire or demolition. Piedmont Hall, at the far lower right, began life as a Methodist church on South Road. It was later moved to Main Street and has since served as an auditorium, a playhouse, a library, and a community center.

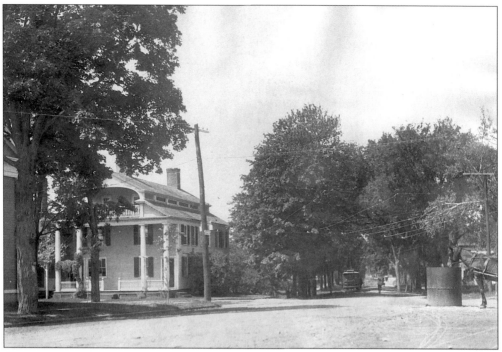

This view of Main Street from Springfield Road looks westward. The trolley car pauses at the end of its run from Springfield via Enfield. At the lower right is a cylindrical riveted wrought-iron horse trough, the occasional bane of automotive traffic.

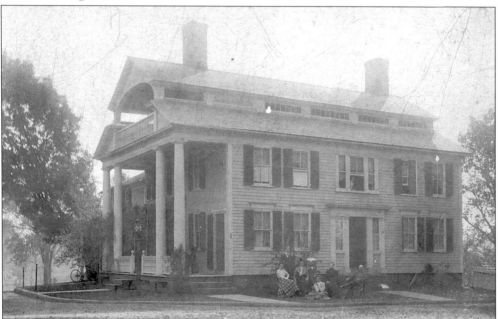

The Fuller-Bugbee house, originally a tavern, stands on the southwest corner of the Route 83 and Route 190 intersection. The Masonic order met in the third-floor ballroom. The lower front rooms served as town offices before the construction of the present town hall. The building was razed in the early 1950s and replaced with a gasoline station.

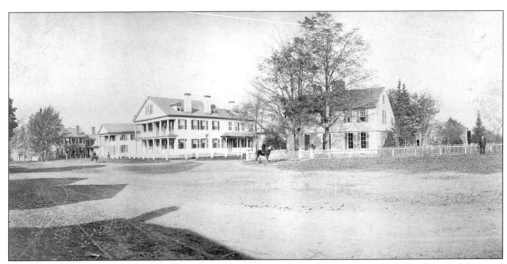

This image looks toward the Kibbe Hotel from the center of town in the 1880s. The saltbox on the right burned c. 1910 and was replaced by an automobile showroom, which later served as a storage facility for the bounty of Somers potato farmers.

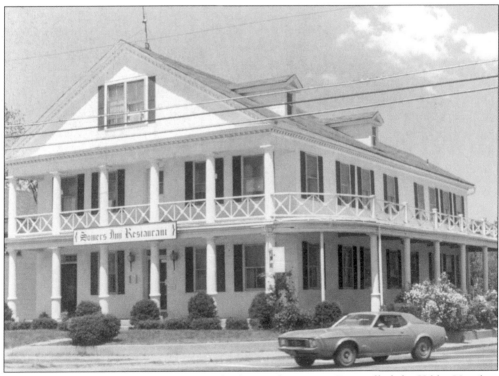

This view of the Somers Inn shows it in the late 19th century. First called the Kibbe Hotel, it was run by Warren Kibbe and then George Kibbe. In 1931, it became the Olde Homestead Inn, run by Alphonse and Hilda Joerg and George and Emmy Schiessl. It was renamed the Somers Inn in the early 1960s.

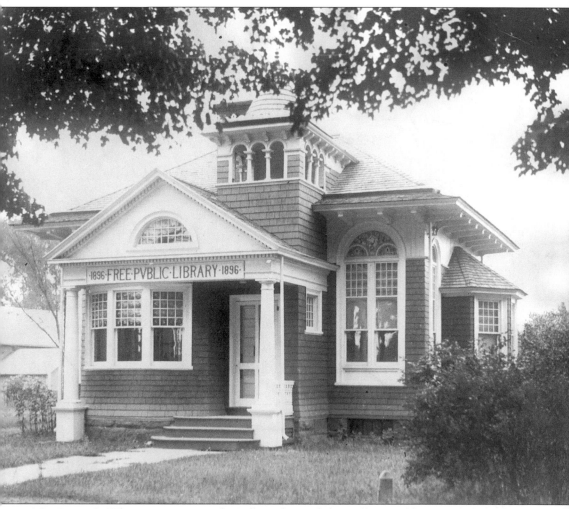

Mrs. James S. Whitney, née Laurinda Collins, donated the Collins Building in memory of her father, William Collins. The building was erected in 1896 on a site donated jointly by W.P. Fuller, C.M. Needham, and N.A. Patten, with concessions by Mr. Needham. With a further donation of $500 by Mrs. Whitney and donations of books from many private individuals, the initial inventory included 1,100 volumes. To make the library more interesting and useful, the directors made provision for the collection and preservation of relics and curios, the beginnings of the museum that the library has become.

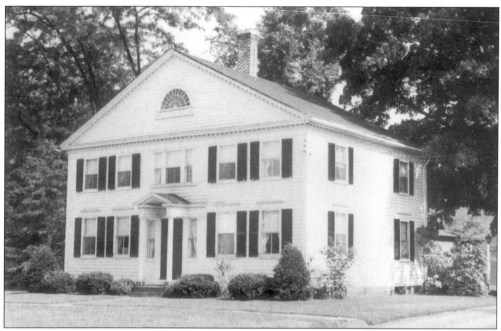

Built in 1805, the house at 568 Main Street was the home of three generations of Hamiltons: Asa, Horatio, and Dr. Erasmus Hamilton. In 1925, Dr. Ralph Thayer occupied the property. The James Shermans restored the home in 1963 and currently live there.

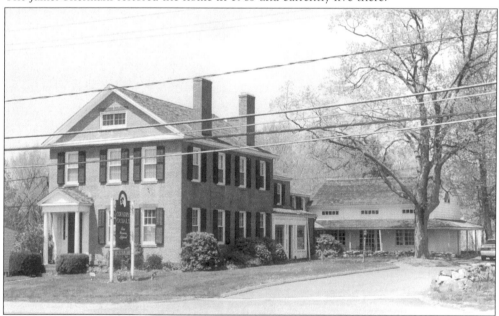

In the early 1800s, Oren Clark and his sons, Ebenezer and Jonathan, lived in one of the earliest brick houses in town at 581 Main Street; they ran the general store next-door. In 1844, it was bought by Rev. Nehemiah Beardsley and occupied by his family for more than 100 years. After passing through several hands as a residence, it was accorded commercial zoning in 1969 and is now operated by Cindy Pio as Country Casuals, selling fine women's apparel. Cindy's family has been in the mercantile trade in Somers for three generations.

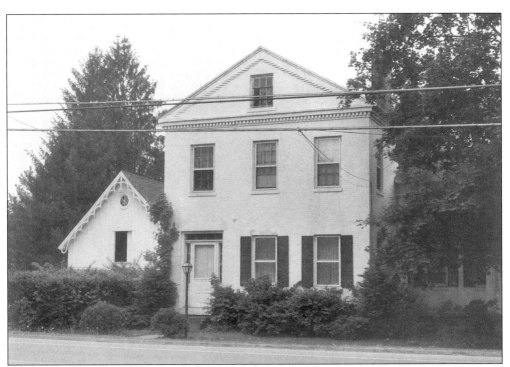

This house at 573 Main Street was the residence of Judge Solomon Fuller (right). He was the first in a dynasty of three judges of probate. Town offices were headquartered in this brick, Greek Revival building that had been painted white. Attorney Donald Shannon lived here from 1955 to 1965 and sold the building to its present owner, Ronald Dudzic.

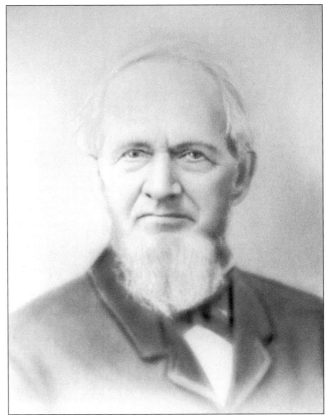

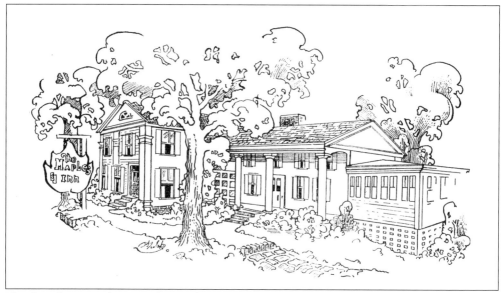

This line drawing advertises the Maples Tea Room at 491 Main Street. The ell was the first part built, early in the settlement of Somers, with the larger two-story section added in 1828. A. Vail Smith, the father of the perennial town meeting moderator of the mid-1950s, owned it in the early 1900s. His daughter, Isabelle Smith Pomeroy, named it the Maples. George Slater ran it as an inn and tearoom until 1953. It has since served a succession of owners as a residence and has been nicely restored, but essentially not altered since its 1828 remodeling.

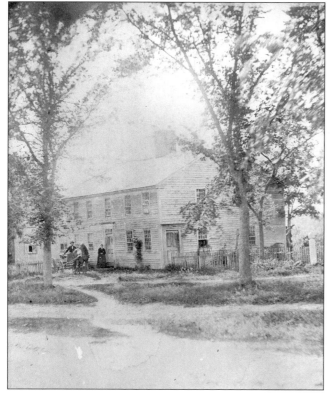

This inn called Elmwood was built at 577 Main Street in 1790. Since 1884, it has been remodeled from time to time to add and then remove a Victorian-style front porch and to redivide the interior. It is now an apartment building.

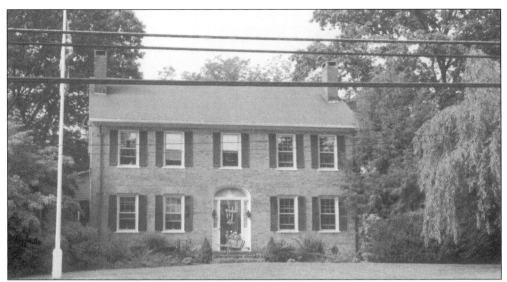

The Nathaniel Parsons House at 521 Main Street was built in 1819. At one time, this lovely old house was used as a tearoom. It was occupied by several generations of the Parsons family and was owned for a while by the Lucius Kibbe family. Walter Whitlock owned it from 1917 to 1943 and called it Arlock. It almost burned down during that time period, but was saved by the Hazardville Fire Department. Shortly afterward, Somers established its own volunteer fire department. Other owners include Hazel Hayes and the Albert Merrill and Rolf Moller families. For many years the bricks were painted white, as was the style of the day.

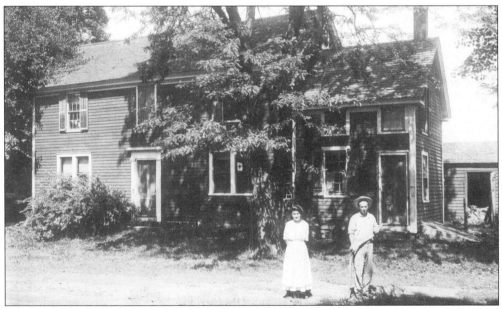

Nathaniel Parsons originally owned this property at 491 Main Street in 1772; it was still owned and being used as a tavern by his great-grandson Ezra Jones Parsons, the son of Samuel and Lucretia Jones Parsons. It remained in the family until 1927. In this picture, the last Parsons family members to own it, Clifford and Grace, stand in front of the home, known as Parsons Tavern. Dean and Miriam Reutter now own the house. (Loan, Dean Reutter.)

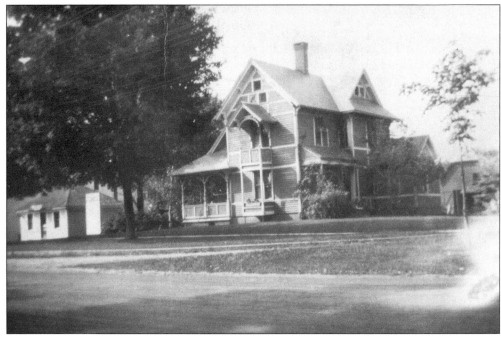

Henry J. Shaw, a Civil War veteran, owned this Victorian house. He sketched scenes around the town and painted the portrait of William Collins that graces the Collins Library. This building and the Sugar Bowl snack shop next-door were razed to make room for the bank and its parking lot.

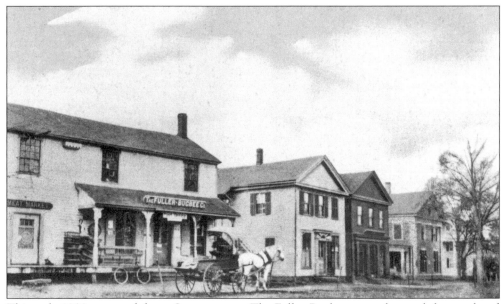

This early-1900s postcard shows Somers stores. The Fuller-Bugbee general store, left, was closed in the early 1930s and removed following damage in the 1938 hurricane. The other stores, with apartments above, were used for various businesses until they were razed for a parking lot in 1976.

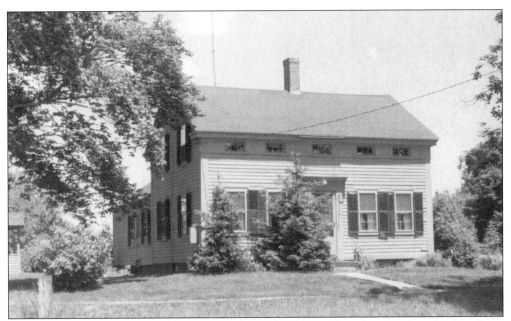

This building, just east of the Congregational church, is said to have been built in 1810, perhaps by Otis Bradley, although the 1869 map shows it as occupied by the Luce family. It was owned by the Bradley family from 1876 until 1953. The church purchased the building from Priscilla and Wilbur Converse in 1972.

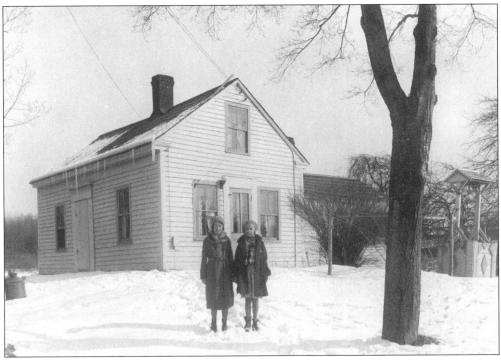

This house was moved from Main Street to its current location at 55 Battle Street. Nelson Eugene Welch, manager of the Somers Creamery, owned it. Here, Ruth Welch poses with her sister Katherine, who still occupies the house. (Loan, Katherine Welch.)

19

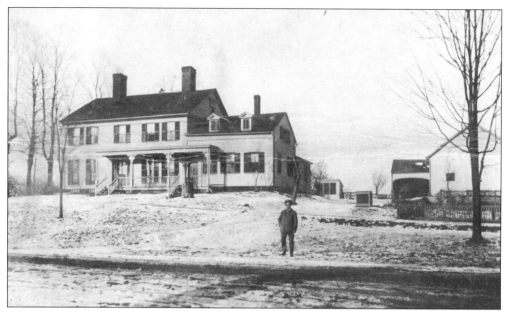

Mary Chapin Pease, the third wife of Claudius Pease, was the second mistress of the Mount Holyoke Seminary. In this 1795 house at 611 Main Street she ran a "select female seminary" called Elm Knoll Preparatory School until her children were grown. Frederick Finley purchased the house in 1925, and converted it into two generous apartments. In 1985, Neil and Debbie Farnham purchased it and converted it into an attractive flower shop. (Loan, Virginia Finley.)

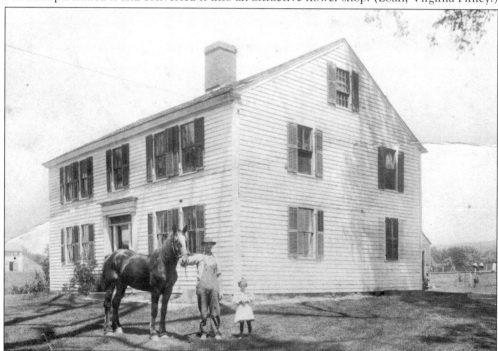

The John Hunt house can be found at 635 Main Street. John Hunt used a horse and buggy to deliver mail for many years. Helen Hunt is shown with Charles Worthington. Several businesses now occupy the building.

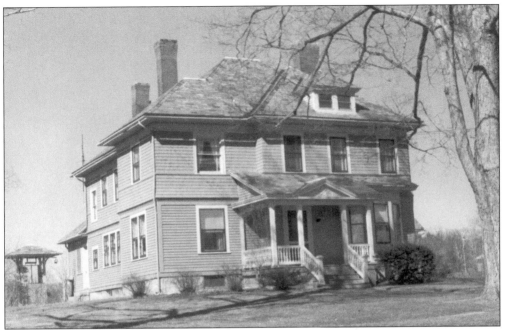

Henry Root Kibbe built Shadow Lawn at 687 Main Street for his son Harry in 1894. The house passed down through the Gager family (Henry's wife was born Mabel Gager) to Cornelius and Rebecca Gager Connell and is now occupied by their son Neil, a local artist.

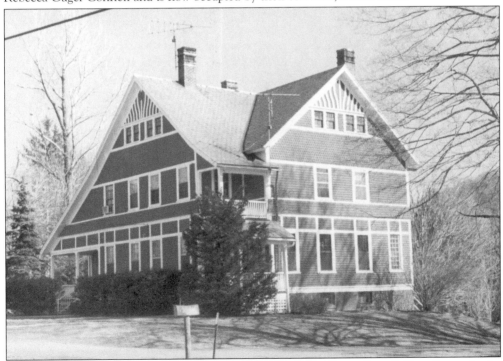

This two-family house at 744 Main Street was also built for Henry Root Kibbe. Currently the Red House Kennels, it is occupied by Donna and Jonathan Davies, who provide boarding and grooming for pets.

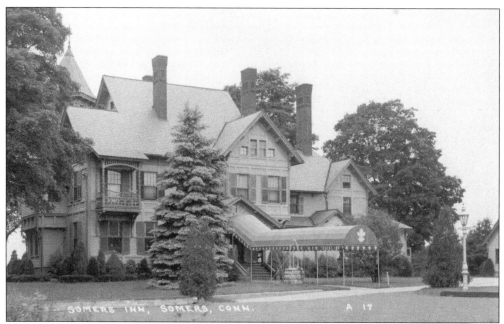

The Henry Root Kibbe mansion Piedmont, the residential centerpiece of a working farm, was built in 1882 and occupied by four generations of the family. Sold in the 1940s, it became the Somers Inn. The present Somers Inn was then called the Olde Homestead Inn. Piedmont was destroyed by a spectacular fire on February 25, 1957. The farm buildings below had been destroyed by fire in 1900. Some years later, Ernest Fuller converted the foundation into a swimming pool.

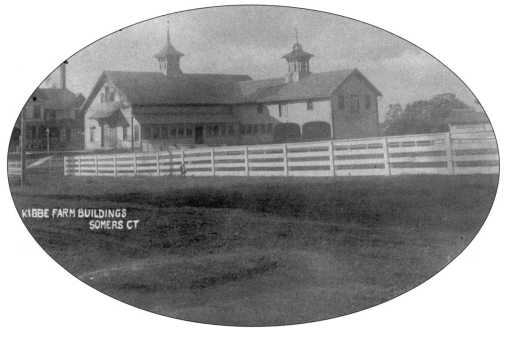

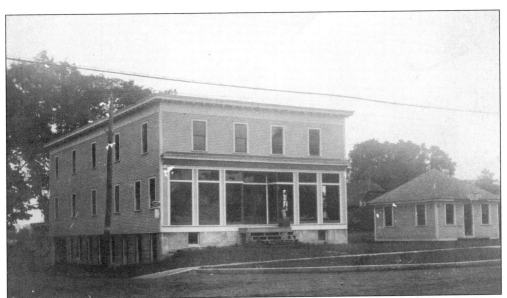

In 1916, an automobile showroom was built at the intersection of Main Street and Springfield Road on a site left open when a Kibbe saltbox house burned in 1910. Later, the building was used for storing and grading potatoes and tobacco; in this use, it deteriorated into an infamous eyesore. The small building to its right is the Sugar Bowl, a snack shop that also housed the post office. In the 1960s, the Connecticut Bank & Trust Company (now Fleet Bank) razed both buildings and constructed the branch bank that now occupies the site.

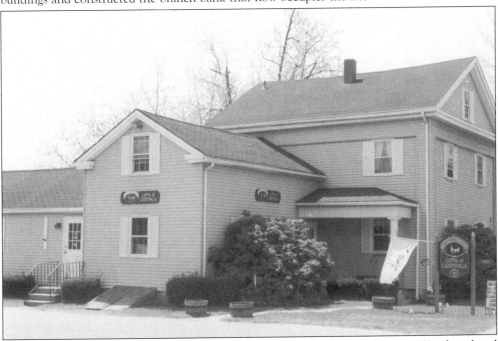

Crossroads, also called the Gold House for its paint, was the home of Marcus Woodward and was built in 1840. This lovely house at 588 Main Street, the intersection of Routes 190 and 83, had been Papers and Presents before it became Crossroads. It is the surviving building in a line of old shops, but it is in danger of being razed.

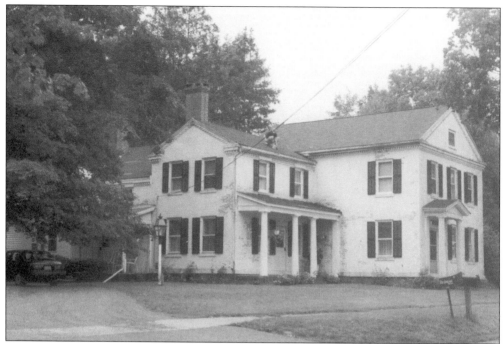

The structure at 41 Springfield Road was built in 1850 by Calvin Hall, a Spiritualist. It was purchased in 1869 by Rev. Erastus Ripley, who established the Select Boys School in a building in a grove behind this house. The school building was moved to Main Street and became the Mechanics Hall. The house was also the home and office of Dr. Alonzo Hurd (1858–1919).

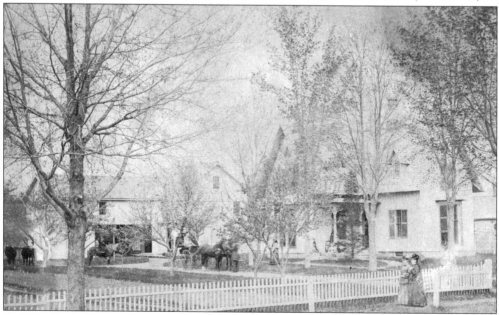

In 1839, Jarvis Kibbe sold Warren Kibbe a large piece of land on the west side of Springfield Road, extending south to Main Street. Warren lived in this Gothic cottage at 33 Springfield Road. He developed a large farm and operated the Kibbe Hotel at the center of town. (Loan, Marianne Myracle.)

24

Two
HOUSES AND FARMS

Somers was largely a farming community with the occasional preindustrial refinements—
sawmills, smithies, and gristmills—that complemented a comfortable, civilized lifestyle.

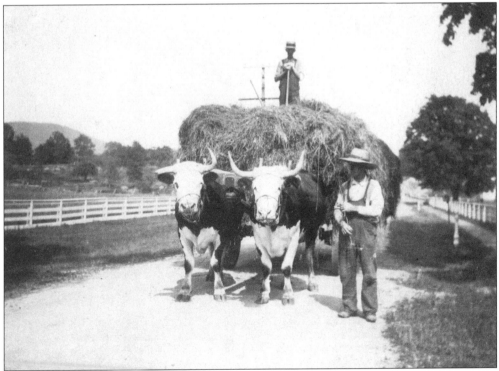

These folks are haying with an ox-drawn wagon on the Piedmont farm, *c.* 1890.

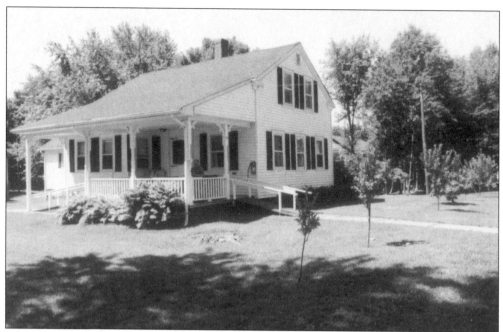

John W. Little bought the land for this house at 92 Main Street in Somersville from Chester Spencer in 1846. Shown here in a recent photograph, the house was likely built by Little, who was a carpenter and joiner. It was sold to the Somersville Manufacturing Company in 1891 and to William R. Taylor in 1969.

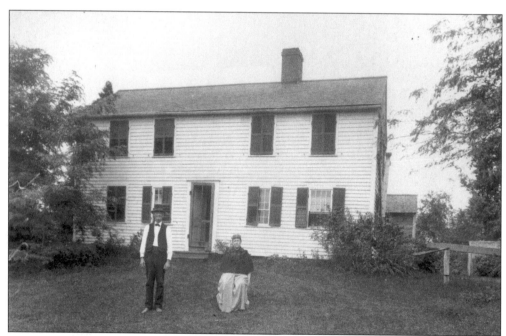

In 1846, Timothy Hulburt sold a house lot at 249 Main Street to Pennel McClure. It remained in the McClure family until 1874. The lady in this picture is not identified, but the man, T.J. Hulburt, lived across the road. (Courtesy of the Ashfield Historical Society, the Howes Collection.)

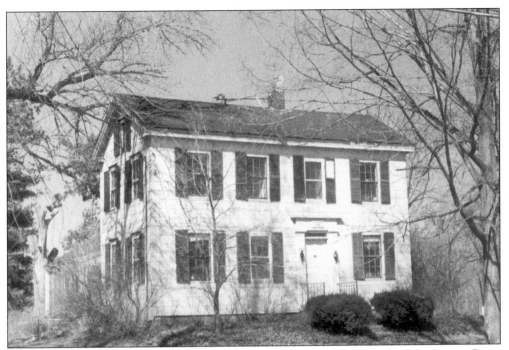

Job Hulburt and his wife, Dorcas Spencer, built this house on the east bank of the Scantic River (299 Main Street). Their son Timothy was living there in 1869. For many years in the 1900s, Fred Davis, a teacher and author of a Somers history, owned this house, which now belongs to Donald P. Smith.

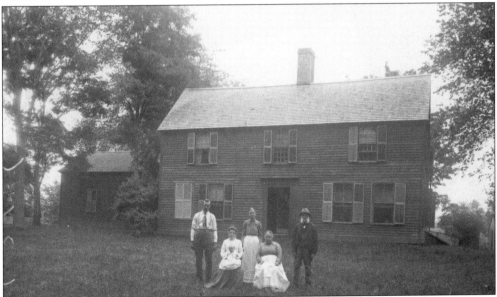

Issacher Jones, kin of Benjamin Jones (among the first four settlers of town), built this house at 332 Main Street in 1745. It was sold in the 1790s to Steven Percival and remained in that family for three generations. It was restored by the Albros family from 1958 to 1960 and is presently the home of Richard Campbell. (Courtesy of the Ashfield Historical Society, the Howes Collection).

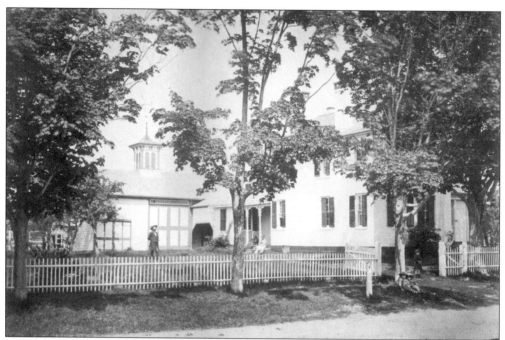

D.H. Schofield lived in this house at 51 Springfield Road in 1857. It was occupied for a time by Captain Wood, the first agent of the Somersville Manufacturing Company. Mary Carpenter Brennan conducted a real estate business from this site from 1966 to 1976. John Doig, the present occupant, has nicely restored the site, as shown below. (Loan, Jude and Carmella Brennan.)

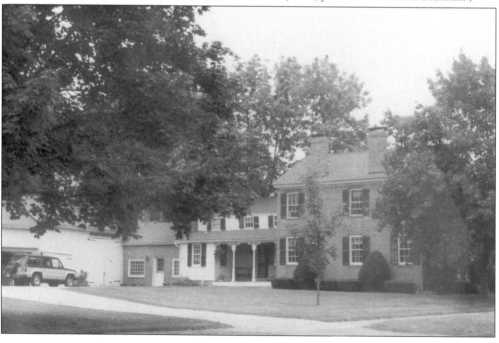

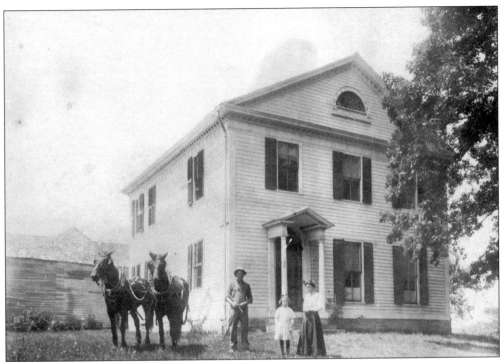

The house at 247 Springfield Road was built in 1808 by Rev. William L. Strong (right), who served the Congregational Church from 1803 to 1829. His son William was twice elected to the U.S. Congress and was appointed chief justice of the Supreme Court in 1860. The house, occupied successively by Solomon Fuller, Randolph Fuller, Forrest Avery, and Ernest Avery (shown above), burned and was rebuilt in 1936.

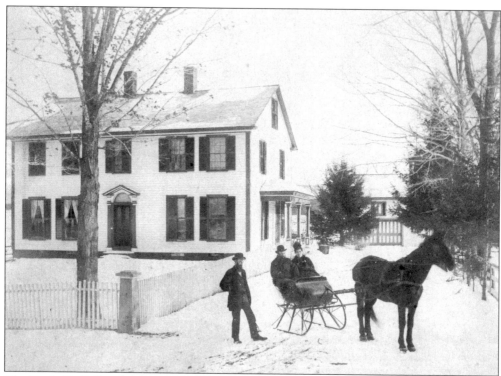

The Noah C. Collins house on Springfield Road was built in 1857 and was later destroyed by fire. Collins had a sawmill and a farm on the property, where it is said Gen. Stonewall Jackson's horse, Little Sorrel, was raised. Shipped to the Union army, the horse was captured at Harper's Ferry and chosen by Jackson. Little Sorrel died many years later at the Virginia Military Institute. The horse was stuffed and was on display until recently.

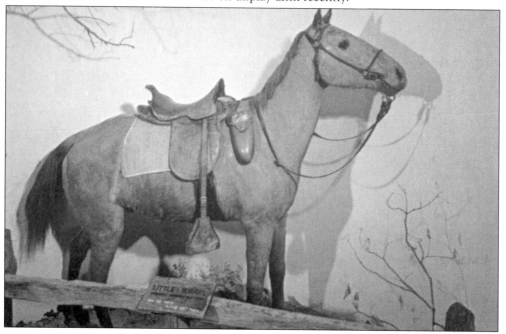

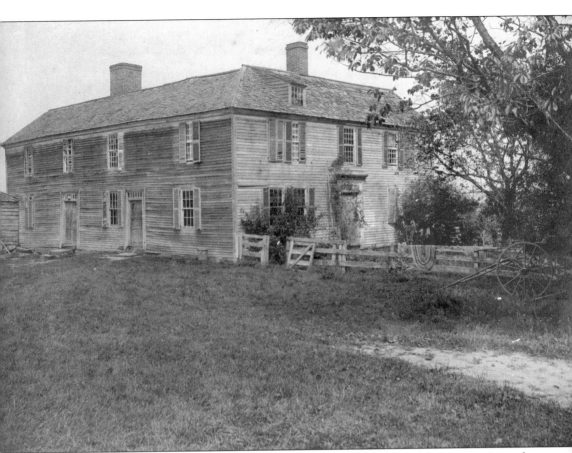

The old Davis homestead, located at the bend in Watchaug Road, housed four generations of the family: Isaac, Isaac, Isaac, and Eber Davis. By 1900, there was no trace of the building. Eber and Lucy's daughter Lomyra married Randolph Billings and, after his death, married Ralph King Jr., in whose Somersville home this picture and other memorabilia were found. Since this picture and one of the Ralph King house (p. 59) were both displayed in a frame with two pictures of the Kibbe Grove Batting Mill, the Davis or the King family may have had something to do with that mill.

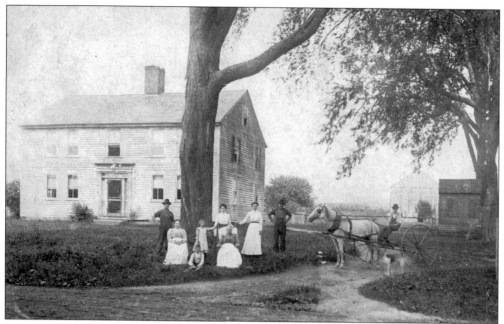

This 1901 Howes Brothers photograph shows the Charles Worthington house on Springfield Road near Durkee Road. It is said that Dr. Charles Backus, an early minister of the Congregational church, held the first divinity school in the United States. He trained many famous men on the second floor of this building, which no longer exists. (Gift, Marie Worthington.)

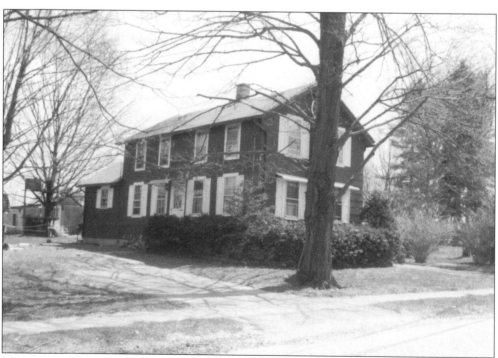

This tenant house at 119 Maple Street was one of two built for the T.M. Gowdy farm. Old Somersville residents believe that Shaker-style bonnets were made in this house.

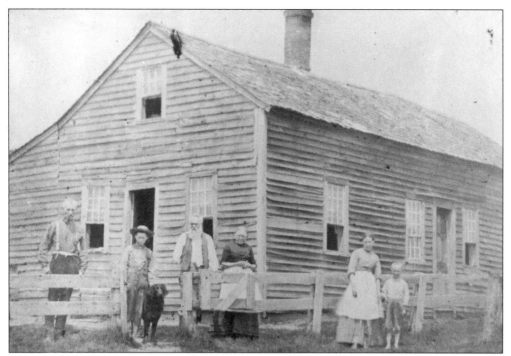

In 1856, George Burbank, son of Daniel Burbank, bought this property at the bend of Hall Hill Road from Julius King. Seen above, from left to right, are Edgar (George's son), William (Edgar's son), George, Artemisia (George's wife), Joanne Collins (Edgar's wife), and Spencer (Joanne's son). This house no longer stands. (Donation, Emma Ferrier.)

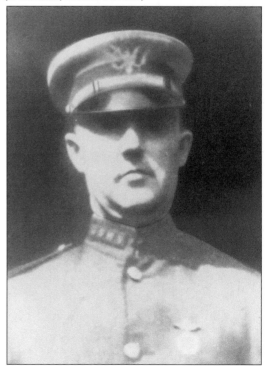

This photograph shows Spencer Leroy Burbank in the uniform of a Spanish-American War soldier.

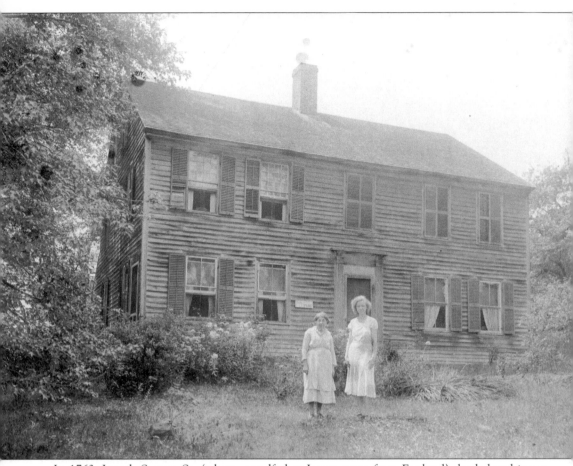

In 1763, Joseph Sexton Sr. (whose grandfather James came from England) deeded to his son Deacon Joseph Jr. this house at 136 Billings Road and property on Abbe Brook (Billings Road). The property passed into the hands of his son Freegrace Sexton and his wife, Anna, in 1800 and thence, in 1853, to their son Chauncey and his wife, Rhoda Pease. Chauncey's daughter Rhoena (left) taught school and was an authority on wild plants. When Gertrude Pinney Wood was over 100 years old, she remembered running cross-lots as a child with a plant for Rhoena to identify. This fine old house has been restored to its original state.

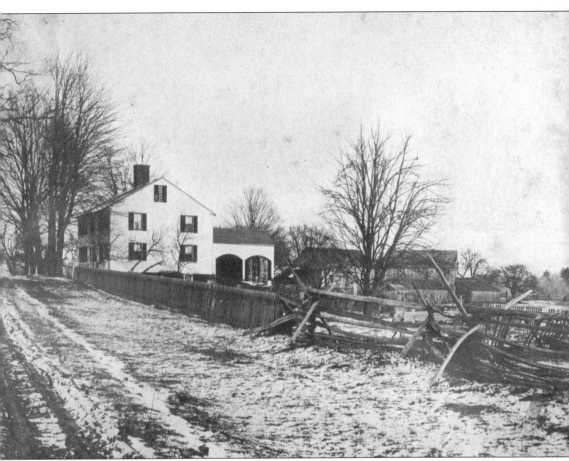

William Collins, grandson of Rev. Nathaniel Collins, came to Somers and built this house at 327 Ninth District Road in the early days of the town's history. It was deeded to his son Joseph and Joseph's wife, Grace Brown, in 1775; their son William was probably born in this house. William married Eunice Parsons, and their daughter Laurinda was born in 1810. Laurinda married James Scollay Whitney and although she moved to Conway, Massachusetts, in her early twenties, she did not forget her childhood home; at the age of 86, she donated the Collins Library in memory of her father. The house was deeded to Daniel Cone Pease in 1832. Daniel's grandson Horace "Junie" Pease was born here before the house was sold to William Hutton in 1936. Dorothy Spellman Hutton, former schoolteacher and Connecticut State Board of Education member, did a tasteful job of restoring the house. After she was widowed, she married Lester Shippee, benefactor of the University of Connecticut. Her granddaughter Nancy and husband, Andy Barrett, are restoring the grounds and raising white-banded cattle on the property. (Loan, Nancy Hutton Barrett.)

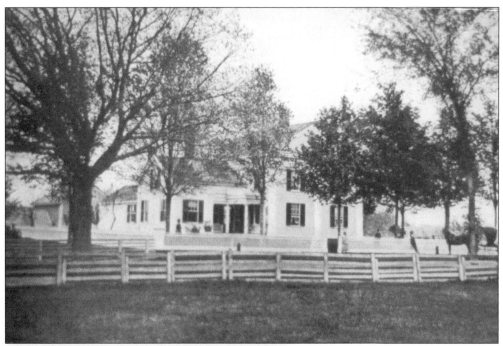

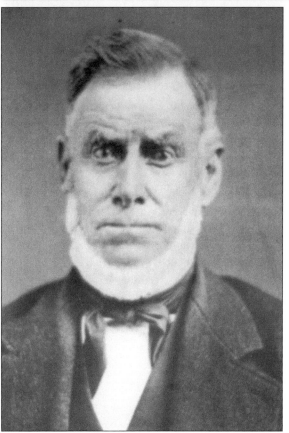

Tudor Gowdy (left) bought a large tract of land from his father, Robert Gowdy, in the 1830s and built this ample house on the east side of Maple Street in Somersville. When the Keeney family moved to this area in 1879, Mayro Keeney, a state legislator and the youngest of Rockwell Keeney's sons, took over this farm and added a cupola. Tom Keeney, great-grandson of Rockwell, occupied the place before selling it to Samuel Palermo, who is maintaining it well. (Photographs courtesy of *Sun Journal*, Lewiston, Maine.)

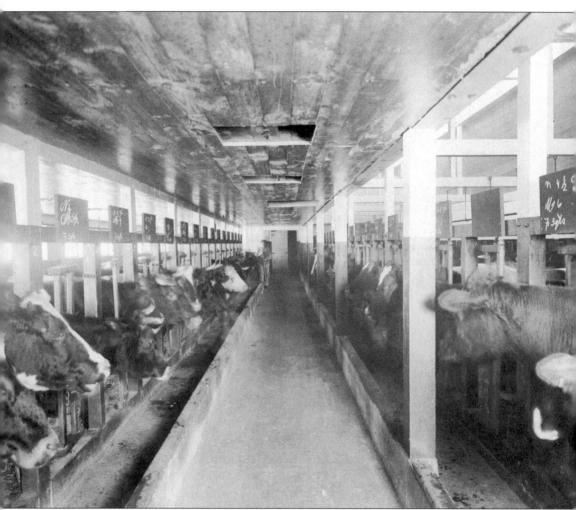

In 1905, Mayro Keeney opened a dairy farm opposite his home on Maple Street. He ultimately had a herd of 60 purebred Holsteins that he stanchioned wide apart in a barn with flush troughs. The farm, specializing in the production of milk for infants, was the talk of the area, although it joined a strong league of dairy farms that pooled their interests in the Somers Creamery. Rosehaven on Turnpike Road was another interesting Somers dairy farm. It was operated by gentleman farmer Henry Root until his death in 1924. Dairying in Somers has taken a distinct back seat to residential land use, and the Root property, owned in the interim by the Gaskells, is under development.

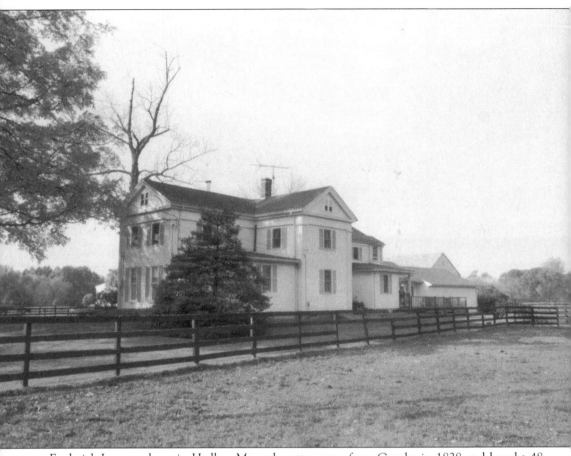

Frederick Loomer, born in Hadley, Massachusetts, came from Granby in 1828 and bought 48 acres from Chester Spencer on the west side of the Gowdy Road, now 100 Maple Street. He built this house and married Dorothy Hulburt, daughter of Augustine. They had four children, Otis, Maria, Origin, and Harriet. Loomer built the blacksmith shop across the road and was Somers's first blacksmith. The land was farmed and remained in the Loomer family until the 1930s. In 1981, the land was bought by Gaetano, Frank, and Gerald Antonnacci, who have developed it into Lindy Farms, a large and prospering breeding and training stable for harness horses.

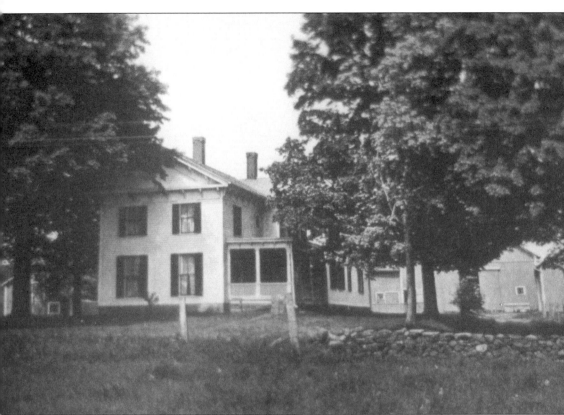

After Myron Gowdy married Harriet Thrall, Tudor Gowdy (Myron Gowdy's father and the son of Robert Gowdy) divided his estate into three parts. The part on the west side of the Gowdy Road (214 Maple Street) was bought "for a fair but nominal price" by his son Myron Fifield Gowdy. A house was built in the transitional Greek Revival Italianate style in 1866; it was described as "a stately mansion composed of the best materials, finished without and within by the best workmen." Myron "filled all the offices in the gift of the town of Somers, save as clerk and treasurer." In 1899, this farm was bought by his nephew Louis A. Gowdy, son of Allen Gowdy and Ellen Fanny Pomeroy Gowdy. Louis was a farmer who held several town offices and served as a state representative; he lived to be 100 years old. Olive Louise Chism was raised here by her aunt Julia Chism Gowdy, the second wife of Louis. The property is now the home of the David Pinney family.

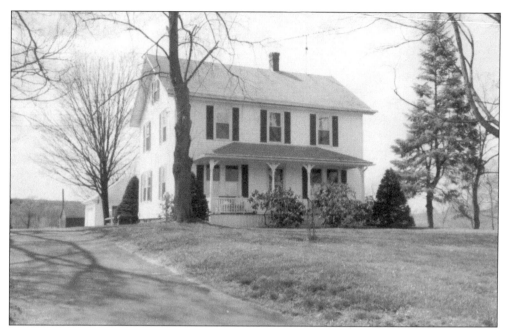

Horace Fuller "Junie" Pease, son of Horace C. Pease and Alta Fuller, was born in 1915 into a long line of Pease farmers. He died in this house at 370 Ninth District Road in 1999. His grandson Roger now lives here.

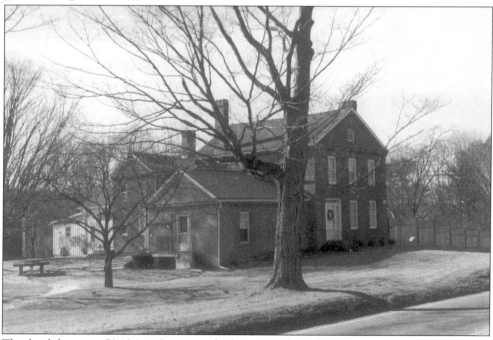

This brick house at 794 Main Street was built in 1838 for Ruby Pomeroy, owner of a millinery shop in Springfield. The bricks were made on the farm from clay carried by oxcart from South Windsor. The bricks had been painted white for a while, but are now the original color. It is known as Olmsted Manor after Arthur Olmsted and has come recently into the care of Rob and Sara Martin.

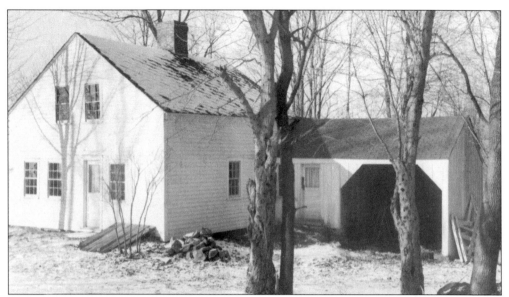

This house at the far end of Scully Road was built in 1780 by Michael Scully, for whom the road is named. Siblings James and Frances Scully lived here in the early 1900s. James, a stagecoach driver, died in 1912. Frances lived alone, though blind, until 1925. The house, renovated in 1959 by A. Vail Smith Jr., has since been taken down. (Donation, Arthur Galbraith.)

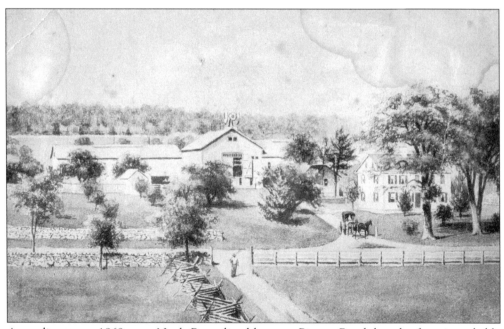

According to an 1869 map, Noah Pease lived here on Pinney Road, but the farm is probably much older. Benjamin Pinney bought this large tract. His grandson Leland now owns it. Benjamin's daughter Gertrude Pinney Wood, born in the original house (which burned and was replaced), lived to be 100 years old. (Loan, Norris Wood.)

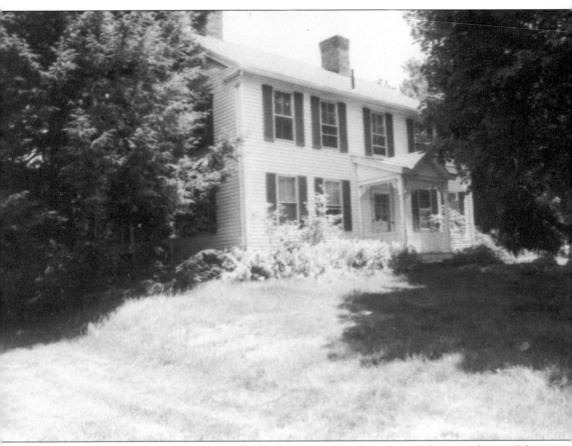

In 1808, Alpheus Billings sold more than 107 acres south of the Scantic River and east of the road to Ellington (1 Pinney Road) to his brother Luke and Luke's wife, Lucy McClure Billings. The homestead was built shortly thereafter, and they had six children. In 1838, Luke sold one-half interest in the property to his son Sanford. By 1876, Sanford and his wife Hannah Russell owned all this property and deeded it to their son William and his wife Mary Gowdy. At this time, Sanford and Hannah moved next-door to raise their three grandchildren, as their daughter Amelia (their only other child to survive to adulthood) had died leaving the three orphans. After William Billings died in 1911, his wife, Mary (mother of his five children), lived in the house ten years before selling the property to Antanas Padegimas, who ran a farm there until his death in 1955. His heirs sold the property to Walter and Guesina Seibert, who sold it in 1987 to Zbignew and Anna Jastrzebski.

Three

EARLY SOMERS SCHOOLS AND CHURCHES

The social infrastructure featured numerous schools to train the children and churches to edify their elders. This chapter will show the growth and modernization of the school system and then add a few images of the older churches. In 1869, there were ten school districts in Somers. Children were expected to walk to the nearest one-room schoolhouse. In the center of Somers and Somersville were larger three-room buildings.

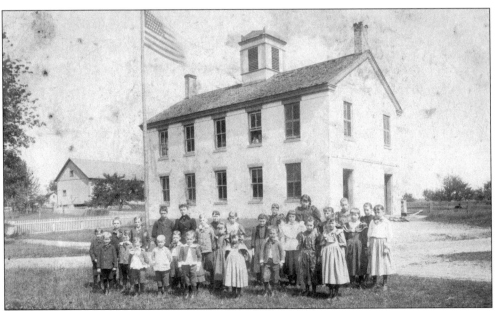

Shown here before 1900, the Somers Center School (District No. 1) was built with brick in 1839. Mabelle B. Avery taught at this school. It was taken down in 1929 to prepare the site to receive the Kibbe-Fuller School. (Loan, K. Welch.)

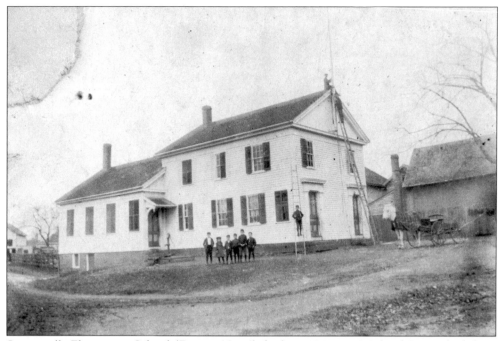

Somersville Elementary School (District No. 6), built in 1844 at 18 School Street, had three classrooms for eight grades. Since more classrooms were needed by 1920, the Spiritualist Hall and the Legion Hall, both across the street, were put into use.

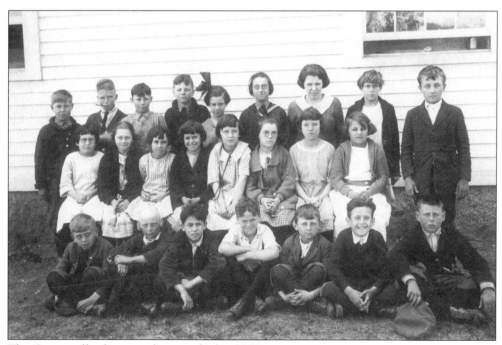

This Somersville class was photographed c. 1900.

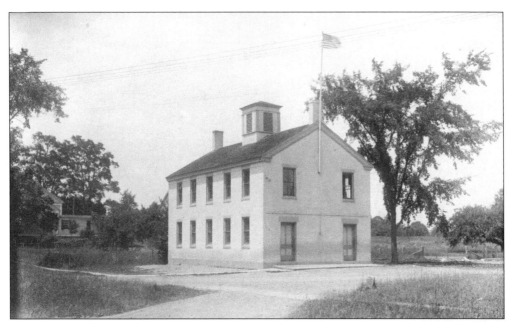

Somers Center School, or the White Brick School, stood where the Kibbe-Fuller School is today. Overcrowding was relieved for a time with the temporary use of two freestanding buildings (one called the chicken coop) before the new Kibbe-Fuller School was built in 1929.

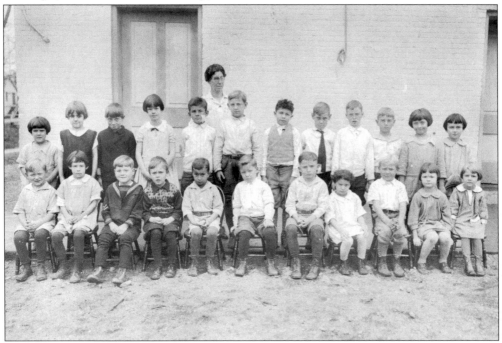

Mabelle B. Avery's Center School class appears here in 1927. From left to right, they are as follows: (sitting) R. Ellis, R. Welch, H. Galbraith, J. Welch, M. Avery, F. Thayer, B. Thayer, F. Lipton, F. Morinski, H. Leroux, and C. Percival; (standing) M. Verrish, A. Galbraith, C. Brunelle, R. Worthington, R. Newsome, S. Lipton, T. Newsome, J. Penocke, J. Lovett, V. Tursin, B. Holmes, and B. Galbraith.

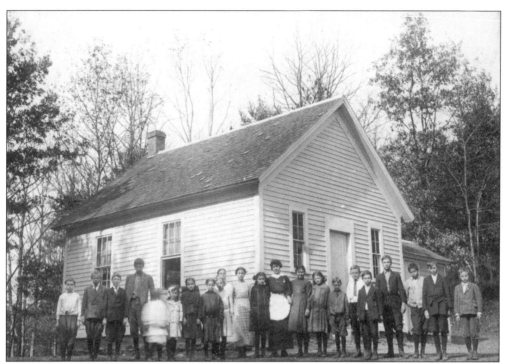

The North School (District No. 4), located at the corner of Hampden and Springfield Roads, is shown above at the opening of the 20th century. It is now a home. The Ninth District School, below, was located at the corner of Ninth District and Billings Roads. Bessie Meacham and Flora King were two of the teachers there. This building was moved east on Billings Road and was made into two small homes, which still stand today.

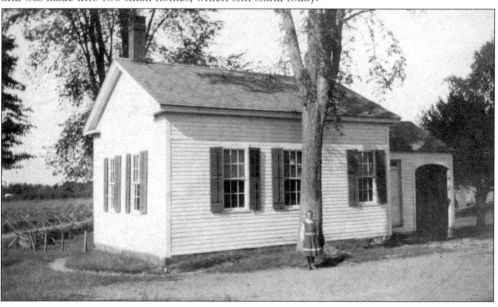

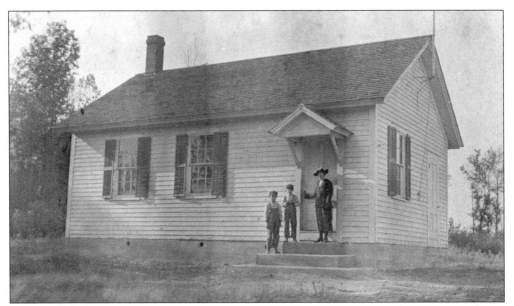

The Hall Hill School (District No. 5) is now a home at 790 Hall Hill Road. The late Martha Butler told of her experiences walking to this school, sometimes skipping atop the stone walls along the roadside.

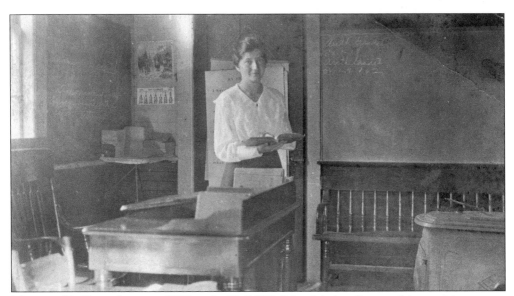

Margaret Griffin is shown in 1917 at the Hall Hill School in her first teaching position.

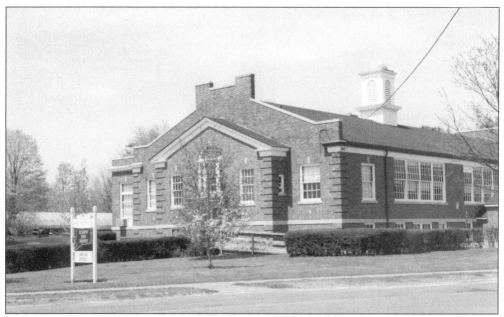

The Kibbe-Fuller School, built in 1929 at a cost of $65,000, replaced the old Center School and others. Judge Ernest Fuller and his wife, Mabel, donated the school to the town in memory of her grandmother, Mabel Gager Kibbe. Closed in 1994, it now houses municipal offices.

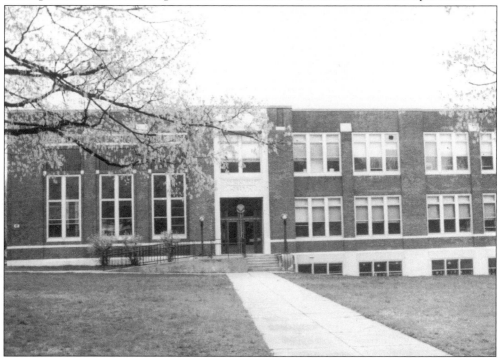

The Somersville Elementary School, located at 18 School Street, was built in 1933 with Works Progress Administration funding. It replaced the old District No. 6 school, the Spiritualist Hall (razed), and the Legion Hall, which was moved closer to the millpond. The building was sold in 1998 to the privately run Grammar School at Somersville.

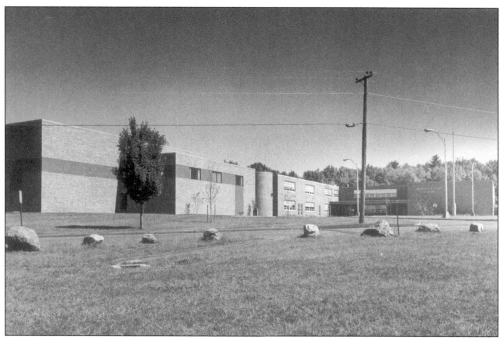

The Mabelle B. Avery School, built in 1966, was named after Mabelle Bertha Avery (1877–1979). Avery began teaching at age 16 in a one-room school and later taught in the Center School and Kibbe-Fuller School before retiring in 1948. She was able to attend the dedication of the school named for her.

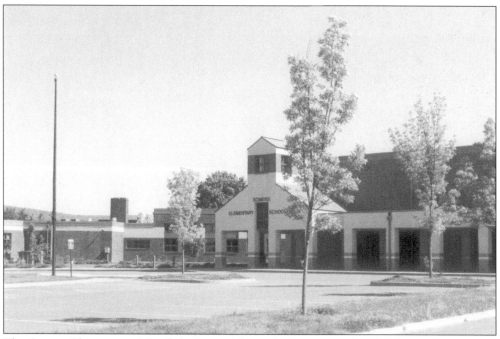

The Somers Elementary School, built in 1958 as the Somers High School, was expanded by additions in 1963, 1969, and 1978. In 1995, after a new high school was built in 1992, the building was remodeled as Somers Elementary School.

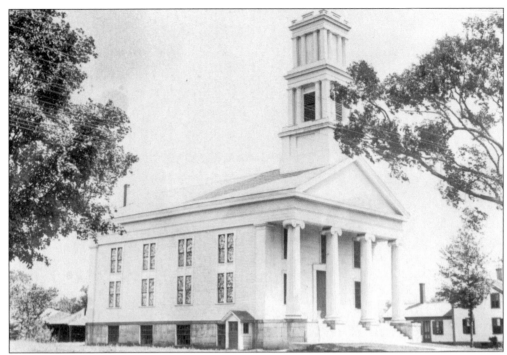

The Somers Congregational Church met in earlier times near North Cemetery—still an interesting antiquarian site. Its third meetinghouse, above, was built in 1842 on Main Street. Early ministers included Charles Backus (1774–1803), who is said to have held the first divinity school in the nation, and Rev. William Strong, whose picture appears on page 29.

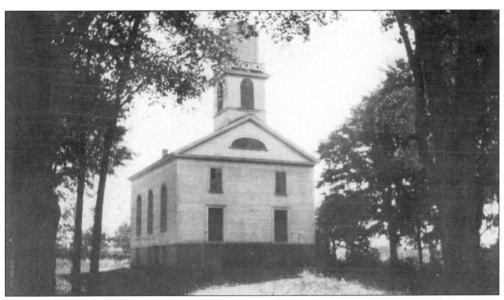

The old Methodist church, built in 1834, was moved several times and was closed by 1900. In 1914, the building was purchased and restored as a community hall by Mrs. Ernest Fuller, who named it Piedmont Hall after her home. It has been used as a summer theater and public library and is today being used again as a community hall.

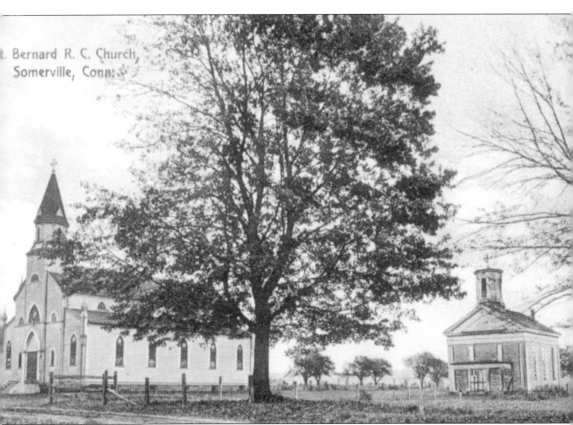

t. Bernard R. C. Church,
Somerville, Conn.

The All Saints Roman Catholic Church, formerly a mission church to St. Bernard's Church in Hazardville, was built in 1897 and enlarged in 1925. Until it became a parish in its own right in 1897, the mission church had used the abandoned Universalist church building that had been moved from Maple Street to this site by 1878. In this postcard rendering, the old Spiritualist Hall stands on the right. It had been a church in Somers near what is now 635 Main Street until it was moved to Somersville in 1883. It served the Spiritualists for a number of years until the building was sold to the Town of Somers for use as a two-room school with the Visiting Nurses Association (VNA) office in the rear. It was used as a junior high school until it was razed in 1933 to build the modern Somersville Elementary School.

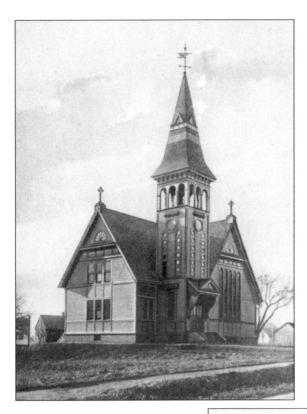

This Stick-style church at 22 Maple Street, a variant of the Queen Anne built in 1878, is the only building in the neighborhood designed by an architect. The Congregational Church of Somersville was initially established with funds that James Billings, the youngest son of Alpheus, put up to be matched. Unfortunately, all the stylistic detail of the building has been covered by vinyl.

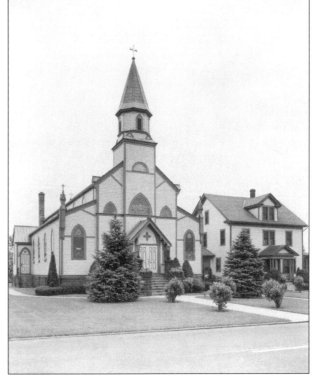

The only example of the Gothic Revival style in Somersville, the All Saints Roman Catholic Church was built in 1897. Most of the parishioners, employed by the mill, were immigrants from eastern Europe, Ireland, and Canada. When the church was named All Saints in 1915, there was a rectory on the site. (Donation, Edward Burgess.)

Four

SOMERSVILLE

At the intersection where several cart paths radiated, "the road to the Gowdys" (Maple Street), "the road to Ellington" (Pinney Road), "the road to Somers" (School Street and Route 190 East), "the road to Enfield" (Maple Street and Route 190 West), and what later became "the road to the Shakers" (Shaker Road) all converged. Samuel Billings came here from Enfield in the 1730s and found the ideal place on the Scantic River for a sawmill, a gristmill, and later a fulling or textile mill. This area was known as Billings Mills before the Revolutionary War and was later called Somersville.

Eventually, these mills changed hands several times and saw good times and bad. In the good times, the owners had built and rented mill houses nearby for the immigrant workers who came from eastern European countries. Skilled workers were lured from England and Canada, and

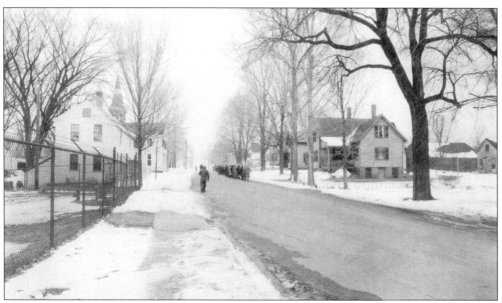

In this image, picketers march up Maple Street during the 1934 strike at the Somersville Manufacturing Company.

homes were built for them along what is now upper Quality Avenue.

The residents who were not farmers were wheelwrights, shoemakers, bonnet makers, and mill workers. Often the farmers too were occupied with one or more of these trades, so through the years Somersville became the mill village of Somers. Since the community had its own school district (No. 6), churches (Spiritualist, Congregational, and Roman Catholic), a barbershop, a post office, and a general store, there was little need to mingle with the residents of Somers Center. With the decline of both farming and mill activity, coupled with the boom in residential land use, occupational distinctions vanished and the people of Somers and Somersville became one. This trend continued in the 1980s and 1990s when a school campus was established off Ninth District Road for all children in town.

Successful men from many fields were residents of Somersville in the 1700s and 1800s. Some of the names included Arnold, Billings, Chaffee, Collins, Gowdy, Hulburt (or Hurlburt), and Pease. In more recent times, many of those names have faded out and the names Keeney, Matero, and Antonnacci have become more prominent. Many farms that once grew corn, potatoes, other vegetables, and tobacco have now become tree farms, horse farms, and berry farms. Tobacco and corn are still successful crops.

Although the vacant mill buildings have become an eyesore, the millpond is still used for boating and stocked fishing. The Somers Beautification Organization has created and maintains several flower gardens in the area, and people have kept their properties in attractive condition.

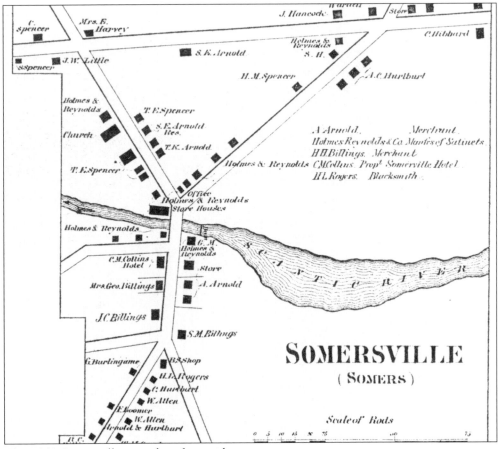

This 1869 Somersville map identifies residents.

54

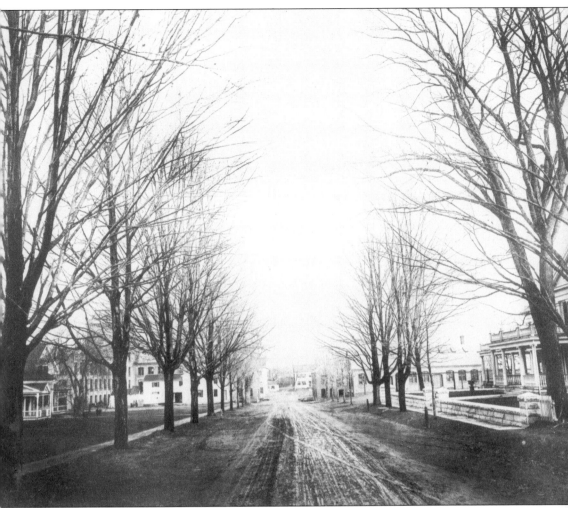

This image looks north from the Blacksmith Shoppe at the intersection of Pinney Road and Maple Street to the intersection of Maple and School Streets. This old picture shows the Lafayette Keeney house on the right and, on the left, the building in which Mrs. George Billings lived, which later moved to Quality Avenue, and the old hotel standing in front of a section of the brick mill building. Alpheus Billings is said to have been born in this hotel building.

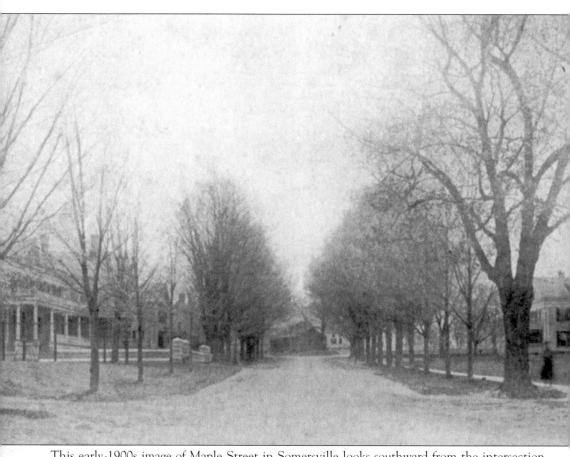

This early-1900s image of Maple Street in Somersville looks southward from the intersection of School and Maple Streets to the Blacksmith Shoppe. Lafayette Keeney's house is on the left and the old hotel is on the right. The woman on the right is Mrs. George Billings.

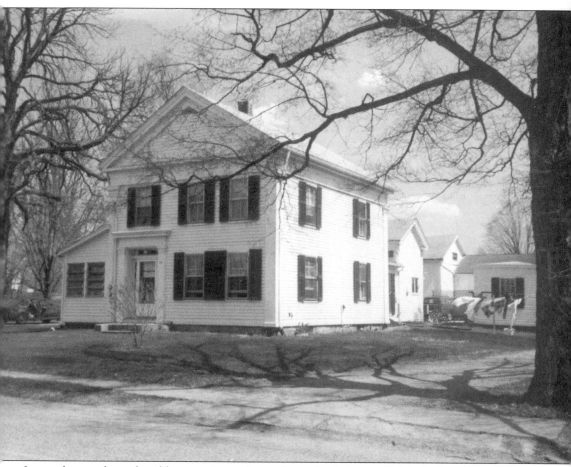

Located on perhaps the oldest continuously run farm, this house at 93 Maple Street was built shortly after John Weston bought land in 1830 from Alpheus Billings and Robert Gowdy. Weston also owned the Wagon Shop across the road. John Tyler owned both properties from 1853 to 1862, when Theodore M. Gowdy (son of Robert Jr.) bought it from the Tyler estate. Gowdy married Jane Billings, daughter of Alpheus Billings, and maintained a large commercial farm. Gowdy was a selectman in Somers for 16 years. The Rockwell Holcomb family bought the property from Theodore's widow in 1915 and ran the farm until it was sold to Henry and Filomena Maturo in 1981.

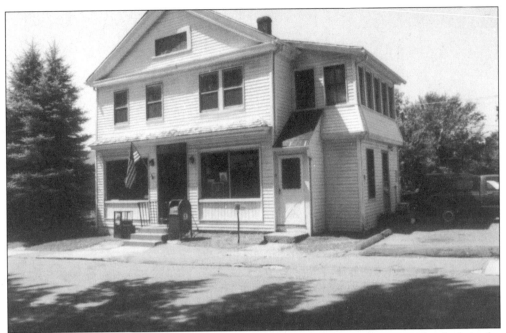

This store and post office was located on Spencer land and was rented out to individuals in the early 1800s. The Arnolds ran the post office until the property was bought by the Keeneys. Still rental property today, it consists of the post office and apartments.

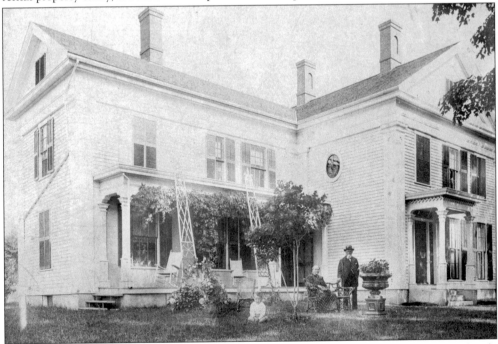

Alpheus Billings lived at 57 Maple Street until his death in 1867. When the Keeney family bought the mill, this house was included in the sale. In 1901, Rockwell Keeney willed it to his son Lafayette, who lived here until 1929. Timothy Keeney, great-grandson of Lafayette, and his wife, Mary, bought the property in 1993. (Loan, Tim and Mary Keeney.)

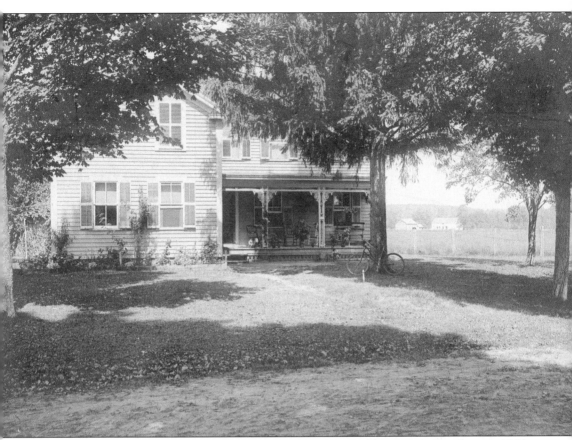

This house, now 128 Maple Street, was built on an acre of land sold to George Meacham in 1864 by Tudor Gowdy, who owned the mansion across the road. By 1868, the same property with house and barn was sold to Randolph Billings, grandson of Alpheus, and his wife, Lomyra (Lovey) Davis, daughter of Eber Davis. They had two daughters—Josie, who died at age 19, and Alice, who later married Mayro Keeney, the man who bought Tudor's farm. Randolph died in 1868 of consumption and, in 1870, Lomyra married Ralph King Jr., son of Ralph Sr. In the barn behind the house, several of the neighbors made wheels, and the Kings, builders of carriages in Hartford, soon moved their business to this location. Three of the eight children of Ralph Jr. and Lomyra King occupied this house for the first half of the 20th century. The girls, Jennie and Flora, were schoolteachers; their brother Howard had a paint shop in the barn. As there were no heirs, the property was sold out of the family. Ronald and Anita Boucher are the owners today.

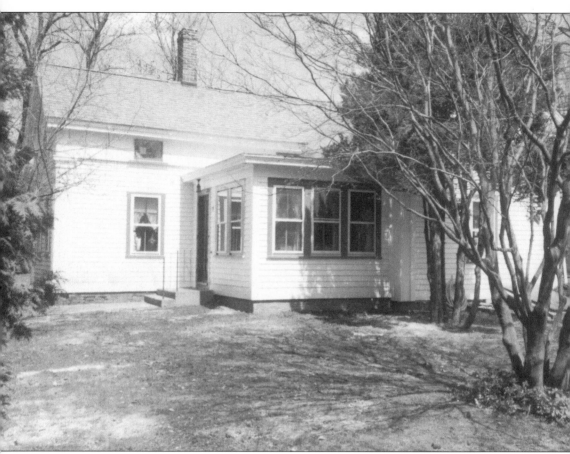

Originally on a large tract of land owned by Alpheus Billings, this small lot at 79 Maple Street, on the east side of the Gowdy Road, was sold in 1840 to Robert Gowdy Jr. and his wife, Anna Henry. They built this house and raised several children. When the children were grown, Gowdy sold the house to Hezekiah Crane, who was his son-in-law and was married to Emeline Gowdy (he had previously been married to her sister Angeline). Leonora, wife of Rockwell Keeney, and Theodore M. Gowdy were sister and brother to these two sisters—all offspring of Robert Jr. and Anna Gowdy. At one time, what is now Maple Street was called the Gowdy Road because there were so many Gowdys living there.

In 1854, Chauncey Hulburt (son of Chauncey) and his wife, Cindonia Gowdy (another daughter of Robert Gowdy Jr.), were living at 79 Maple Street with their daughter Lizzie. In 1934, when Lizzie died, her will provided money to place sidewalks throughout Somersville. Some of the old-timers remember this, as it became a fine place to roller-skate. Chauncey Hulburt was a wheelwright who worked with his brothers, Samuel and Irwin, at the shop on the other side of the road between the Loomers' and Randolph Billings. In 1934, James Wood, who had come from England to be a mill supervisor, owned this property. His son J. Francis Wood also became a mill foreman. Celia, daughter of James Wood, lived here unmarried until her death in 1963. There have been at least four families in this house since 1963.

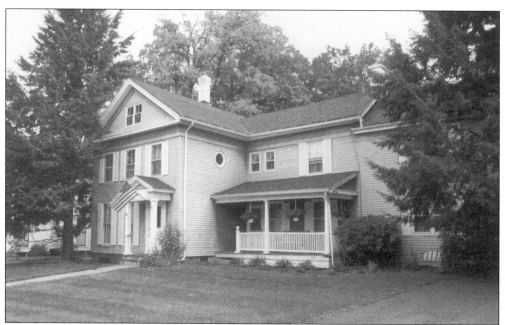

This original two-story, gable-to-street residence at 63 Maple Street was built in 1860 by Ansel Arnold for George Converse and his wife, Amelia Billings Converse (daughter of Sanford Billings). When Amelia died, leaving three children orphans, Sanford and his wife, Hannah Russell, left their farm next-door to their only living offspring, William Billings. They moved here to raise their grandchildren. Later, George Homer and his wife, Mary Denison (sister of the wives of Lafayette and George Keeney), lived here while he ran the store at the corner of Main and Maple Streets. After World War II, Robert Keeney Jr. (grandson of Lafayette Keeney) raised a family here and enlarged the house to accommodate his growing family.

In 1986, Ralph and Phyllis Lumb saw a potential for a bed-and-breakfast operation in this mansion and bought it from the heirs of the Robert Keeney estate. After putting in a driveway, several parking spaces, and a two-car garage, it opened as the Old Mill Inn at 63 Maple Street with the sign that appears on the right. The inn was sold c. 1993 to avid would-be bed-and-breakfast operators James and Stephanie D'Amour. The D'Amours continue to provide comfort to travelers.

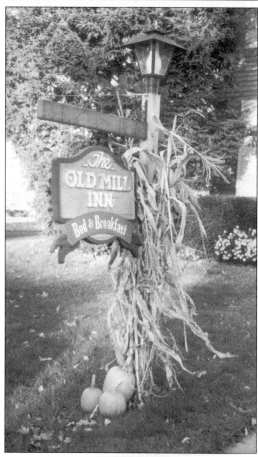

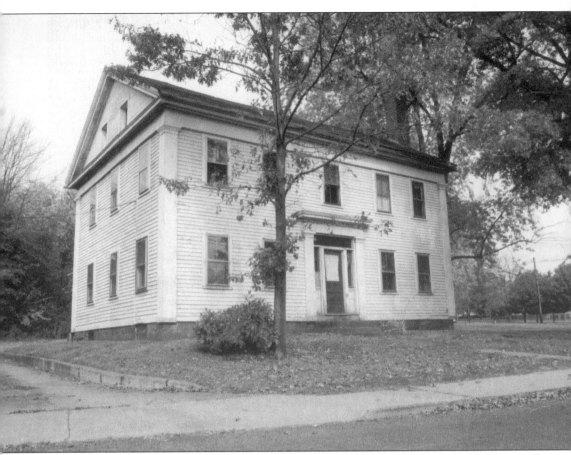

This Greek Revival–style house at 39 Maple Street has had a long association with Somersville mills. Built by Samuel Billings, the first owner of the Billings Mills, the house is shown on page 86 in one of the earliest pictures of the mills before the brick building was added in 1835. In 1840, it was sold to the Spencer-Chaffee operation. It was transferred from the Chaffees to Holmes and Reynolds & Company in 1853 and then to Rockwell Keeney and his sons George and Lafayette, the founders of the Somersville Manufacturing Company, in 1879. According to Keeney descendants, it was the home of Rockwell Keeney until his death in 1901. After that time, it was used as a boardinghouse and personnel office. The rear addition eventually housed the company's fire department in the early 20th century.

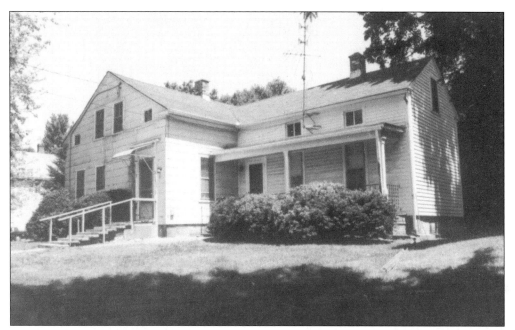

Asa Hamilton Spencer, son of Chester Spencer, occupied this house at 19 Maple Street by 1828. Originally on Billings's land, it remained in the Spencer family until 1938, when Mandana Spencer sold it, but she lived in the ell rent-free. In 1963, it was sold to the Follansbee family, who sold it to Jack and Mavis Collins in 1984.

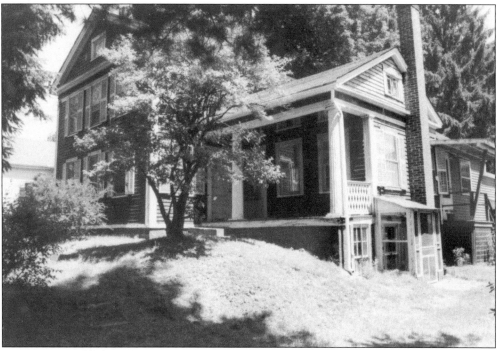

Henry Pease sold this property at 25 Maple Street to Samuel Arnold. For 100 years, Arnolds lived there, maintaining the two tenant houses to the south of them. For many years, Emily Arnold Standish and her daughter, Inez, were postmasters at the post office across the street.

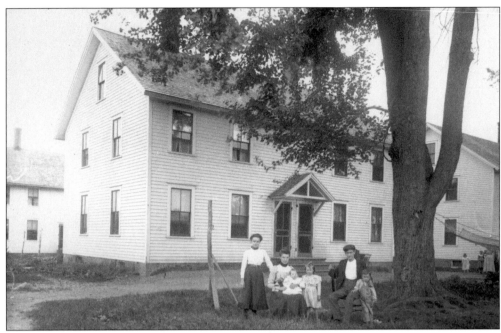

These two houses are examples of tenant houses, built by Holmes and Reynolds & Company to be rented to their mill employees. The picture above shows a tenant house on the south side of Main Street. The picture below shows a mill house on School Street. (Above, courtesy of the Ashfield Historical Society, the Howes Collection.)

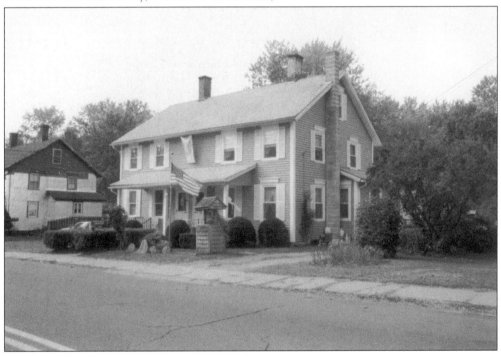

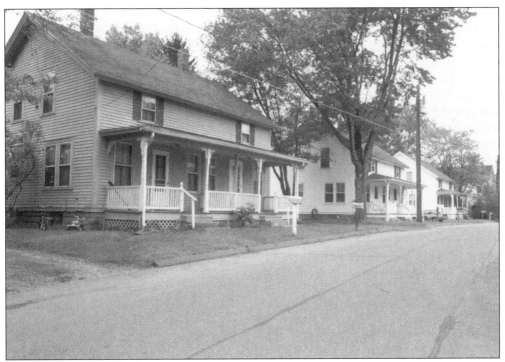

Two different styles of tenant houses, duplexes and apartments, are located on Quality Avenue. They were built by the Keeneys of the Somersville Manufacturing Company in the early part of the 1900s.

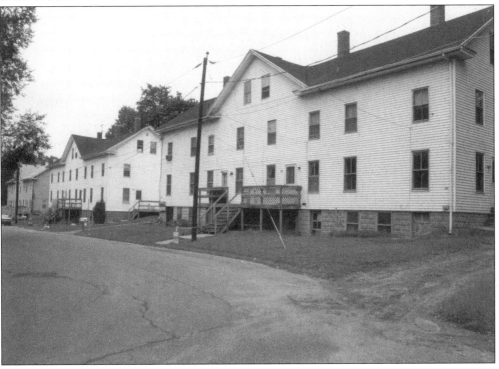

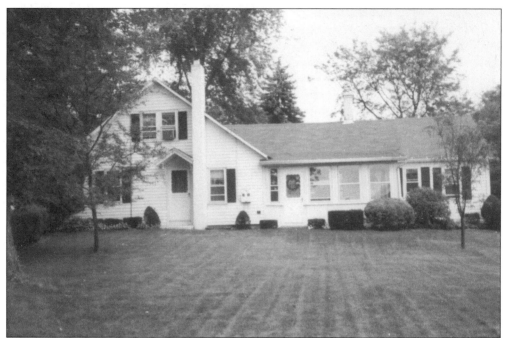

The earliest part of this house at 8 Shaker Road was built by Cyril Chaffee (1758–1837), who came from Woodstock, Connecticut. His grandsons William and James Chaffee, with their uncle Chester Spencer, did business as Spencer & Chaffee and ran the mills before Holmes & Reynolds.

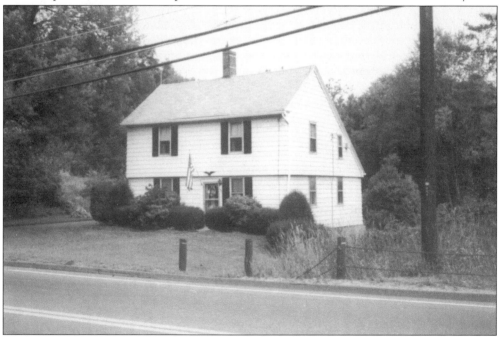

Probably the oldest saltbox in Somersville, the house at 45 Main Street was occupied by Ebenezer Spencer before 1739. Just west of Coronation Brook, now Woods Stream, it was in the Spencer family until James Wright bought it in 1864. The Wright family owned it until 1941, when the Heberts bought it.

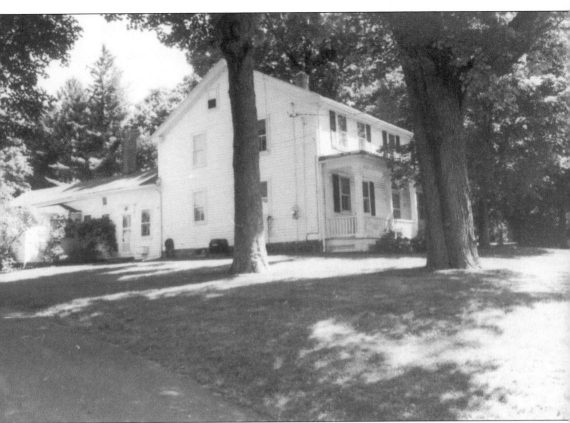

This house at 79 Main Street, one of the earliest still standing in Somersville, is historically significant for its association with the Spencer family. It was built for Ebenezer Spencer Jr. *c.* 1760 on land he inherited from his father, Ebenezer Spencer. In 1793, Ebenezer's brother Ezekiel bought the 10-acre farm with dwelling house and barn. Ezekiel's son Chester was the owner according to the 1869 map of Somers (p. 74). He was a dry goods store owner when he married Hannah Chaffee in 1831. In 1835, Hannah's nephews, William and James Chaffee, entered the manufacturing business with Chester Spencer under the firm name Spencer & Chaffee. They bought out the early mill privileges of the Billings family in Somersville and built a satinet mill on the Scantic River, the later site of the Somersville Manufacturing Company.

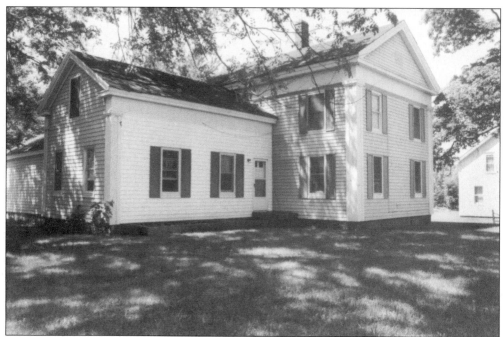

The house at 74 Main Street is composed of two main sections built some 20 years apart. Samuel Spencer built the one-story part *c*. 1800. By 1869, his son Samuel was living there and the two-story Greek Revival–style addition was in place.

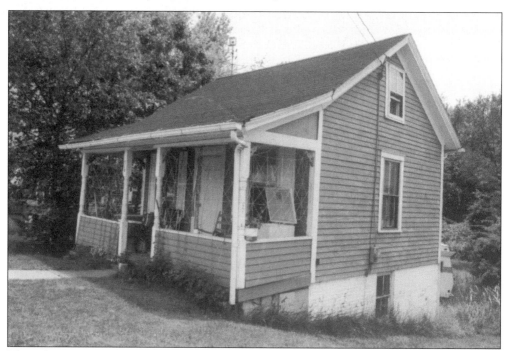

The John Spencer Barber Shop at 118 Main Street was one of the few historic commercial buildings in this section of Main Street in Somersville. It was built *c*. 1900. John Spencer and his wife, Malvina, built a dwelling house and a shop on this property and ran it for 20 years.

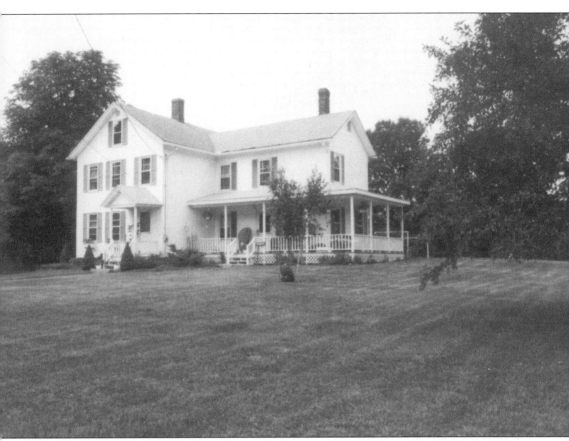

After her husband's death in 1881, Bridget Delaney, one of Somersville's more enterprising women, borrowed enough money to buy an acre of land from Elizabeth Chaffee Harvey. Delaney built this house at 129 Main Street as a boardinghouse. She and her husband had come from Ireland to New York City and then to Somersville, where he was a laborer at the mill. In 1901, the property was deeded to the youngest daughter, Lizzie, providing she live at home during the lifetime of her mother. Bridget died in 1910 and, in 1929, Elizabeth Delaney Perry sold the property to Alexander and Mary Olisewsky. In 1966, the estate went to Alexander's daughter Susan Waniewski and is still in that family.

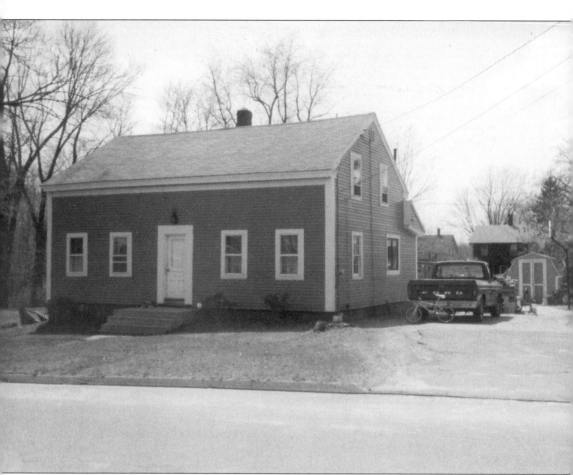

This small house was originally located just south of the Somersville Manufacturing Company on the west side of what is now Maple Street. The 1869 map shows Mrs. George Billings, daughter-in-law of Alpheus Billings, living there. It had been sold with the mill to the various owners over the years until early in the 1900s. When Leland Keeney, grandson of Rockwell, decided he wanted to build his home on that site, he elected to move the house to Quality Avenue. Old Somers residents remember it being moved north, across the bridge, to what is now Quality Avenue, over Wood Road, which was just south of the Congregational church. Here, J. Francis Wood (foreman of the mill) and his wife, Gertrude Pinney Wood, lived for many years and raised their family. Michelle Michals is the current owner of 24 Quality Avenue.

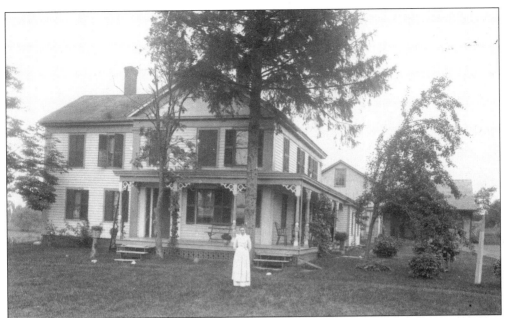

In 1833, Solomon Billings bought this property at the intersection of two major highways in Somersville (Route 190 and Hall Hill Road) and built this house. His sons, Horatio and Horace sold this house and 110 acres to Alpheus Hulburt, who passed it down to his daughter Maria and her husband, Richard Delaney. In 1945, the estate was left to Richard's son Chester Delaney, who lived there until he sold it in 1961 to Robert and Patricia Parks. In 1985, it was sold and several owners have used it for business offices since. At one time, several small stores were to the left of this house, near Hall Hill Road. Below is an aerial view of 179 Main Street, the Delaney house. (Above, courtesy of the Ashfield Historical Society, the Howes Collection; below, donation, U.S. Dzwonkus.)

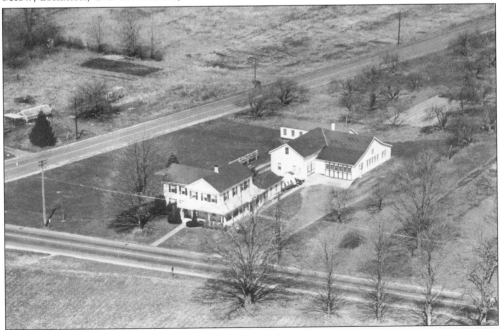

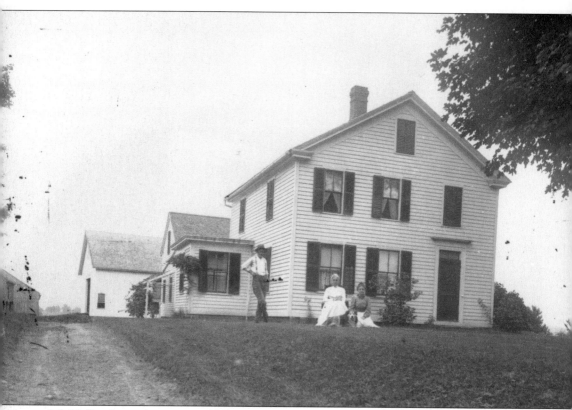

Job Hulburt's son Augustine sold this property in 1832 to his nephew Alpheus Collins Hulburt, son of Job Jr. Alpheus, whose mother was Lucinda Collins, had married Lucinda Williams in 1832. They lived here until 1866, when his son-in-law Charles Hibbard took possession. Between 1909 and 1929, several families had lived here until Jesse and Elsie Goodwin bought it and farmed the 50 acres. By 1971, the acreage had been sold and subdivided as Goodwin Drive, and Raymond and Sally Sargent had bought this house at 260 Main Street. (Courtesy of the Ashfield Historical Society, the Howes Collection.)

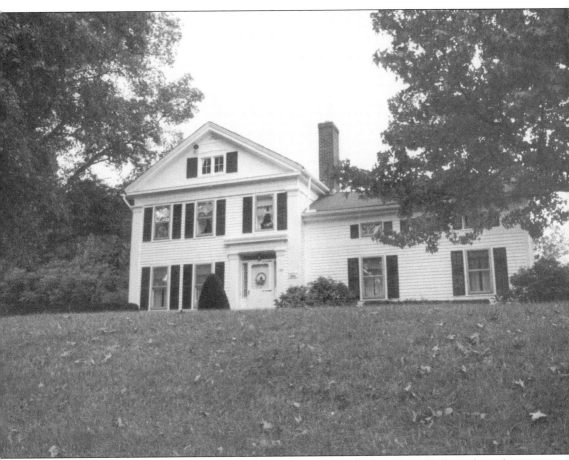

This Greek Revival building at 193 Main Street was the home of Solomon Billings (grandson of Samuel) after it was built in 1850. In a remarkable 1860 indenture, which has survived in the land records, he leased all the property (including the homestead) to Horace and Horatio, his youngest sons, whose ages at that time were 47 and 48, respectively. In return, his sons agreed to provide "suitable meat, drink, clothes and lodging" during the natural life of Solomon, or if he wished to live elsewhere, to pay board for his care. In 1865, his estate sold the property to Loren Griswold, who lived there until his death in 1906. It was sold at a bankruptcy sale to Herbert Thatcher, whose son Harold sold it to R. Leon and Thelma Smith in 1946. Today, the much-traveled Thelma still entertains with her illustrated travelogues.

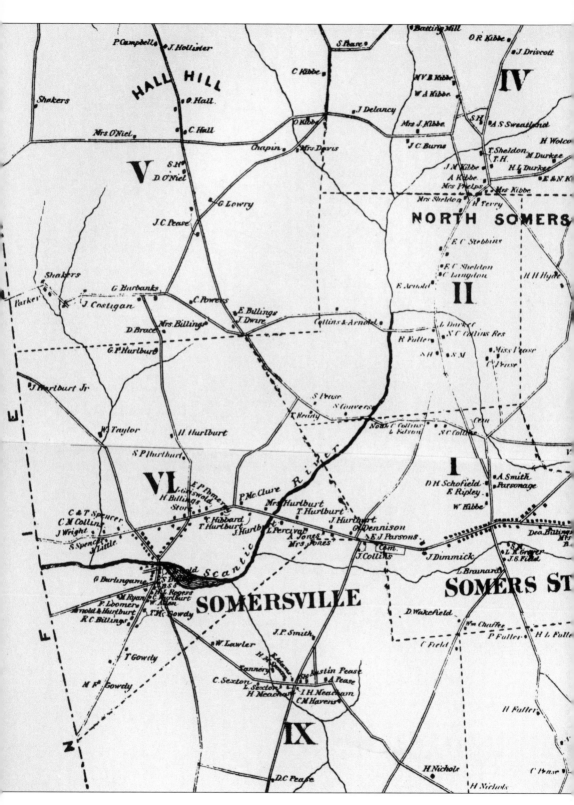

74

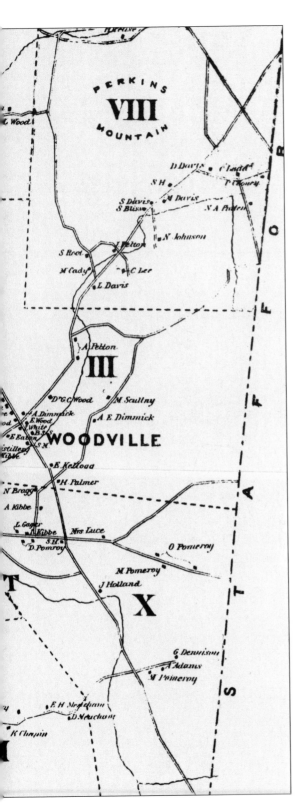

This Baker & Tilden's map of Somers (detail) was compiled in 1869.

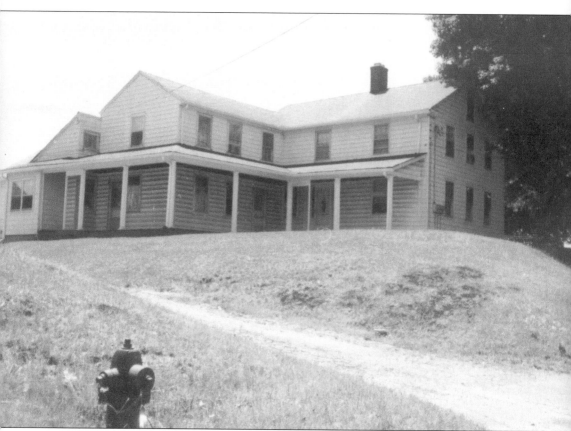

There was a dwelling at this location at 260 Main Street in the early 1800s, when Daniel Webster of Longmeadow bought it. Webster sold this property to Theodore Hulburt, son of Captain Job, in 1862. It passed down through three generations—Theodore, Edwin, and Theodore J. Hurlburt—until it was bought by the Maturos, who still have a farm here.

Five

BUSINESS AND INDUSTRY

On the 1857 map of Somers, there appear to be many businesses. Stores sold all necessary supplies, and various shops employed the residents. These included smithies, carriage shops, tanneries, gristmills, sawmills, a harness shop, a bonnet shop, satinet mills, woolen mills, and batting mills, each with its own skilled workmen.

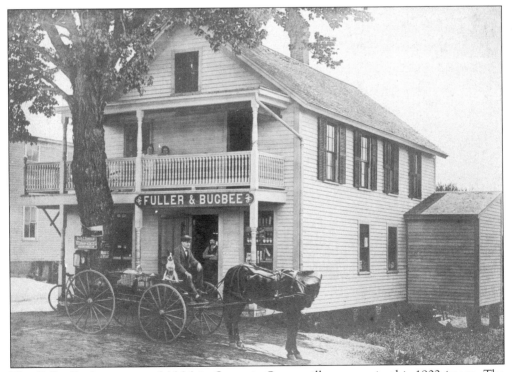

The Fuller-Bugbee store at 146 Main Street in Somersville appears in this 1902 image. The business later moved to Somers. Etta Fuller Bugbee sits on the porch, while her husband, Raymond Bugbee, drives the delivery wagon.

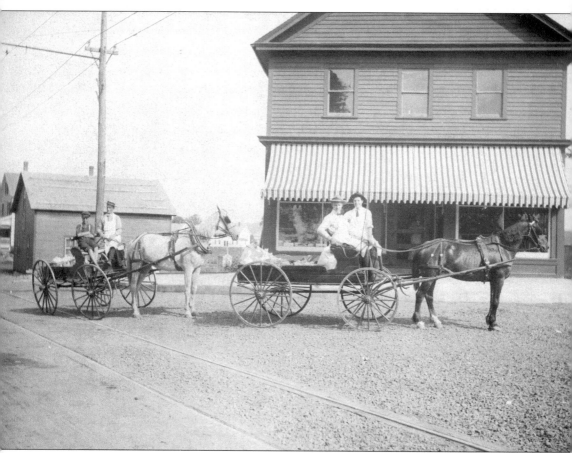

Homer's Store stood on the corner of Main and Maple Streets in Somersville. In this 1913 picture, two delivery wagons are shown. Employee Frank Connell drives the one in the rear, accompanied by his son Bucky. In the basement of this building was an ice-cream manufactory, which used ice that was cut from the millpond and stored in an icehouse on the property. George Homer came to Somersville with the Keeneys and rented 63 Maple Street as a residence. George's wife was sister to the wives of Lafayette and George Keeney. George bought the large corner lot from Dorothy Spencer and built the store in 1901.

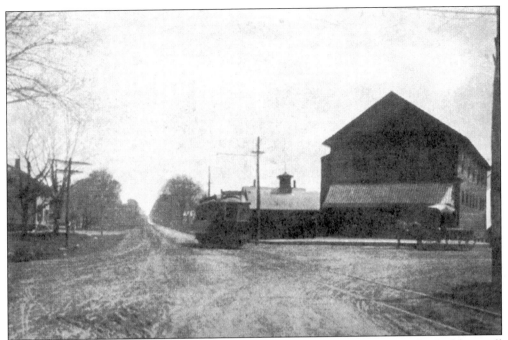

This photograph shows Homer's Corner in 1914. Note the trolley. Today, the building still stands, but this façade has been closed, and businesses on the ground floor are accessed from the Main Street side of the building.

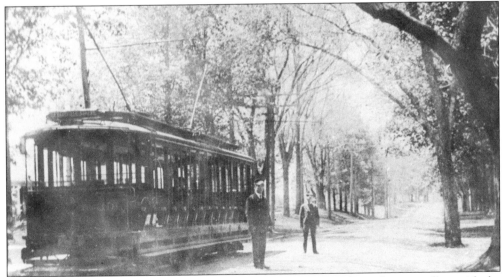

This view of the center of Somers looks west. A Connecticut Railway electric trolley, with the conductor and motorman standing outside, pauses at the end of its run from Enfield. This trolley carried high school students to Enfield and delivered milk from the Somers Creamery for processing in Springfield.

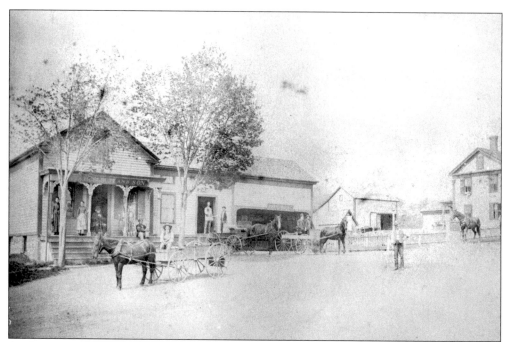

At the corner of Hall Hill Road and Main Street in Somersville stood several stores that are now gone. The 1869 map shows the H.M. Billings store, enlarged by the time of this picture to include a feed and grain store and a blacksmith shop. Richard Delaney continued these businesses, and his son Chester provided school bus services to the town.

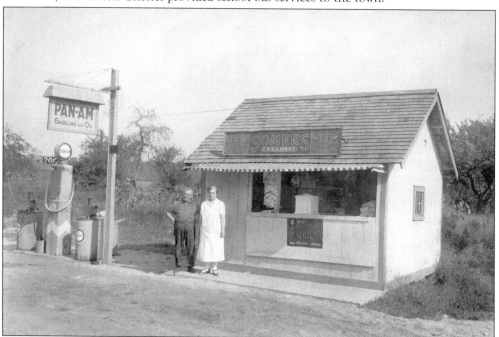

Mr. and Mrs. Fred Brunell stand in front of their gas station and ice-cream store on the corner of Main Street and Sokol Road in 1926. As you can see by the sign, the ice cream came from the creamery. This building is still standing.

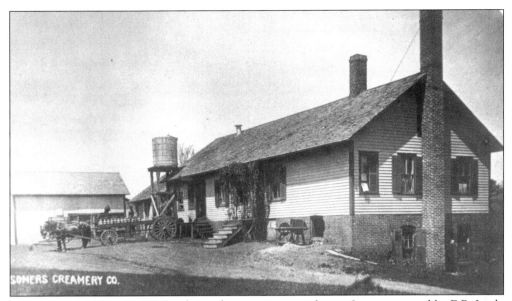

The Somers Creamery at 32 South Road is now a private home. It was operated by E.B. Little and later by a Mr. Cushman. Milk was collected locally and ice cream was made and transported by trolley to Enfield. The business was purchased by H.P. Hood & Company and moved to Springfield in 1925.

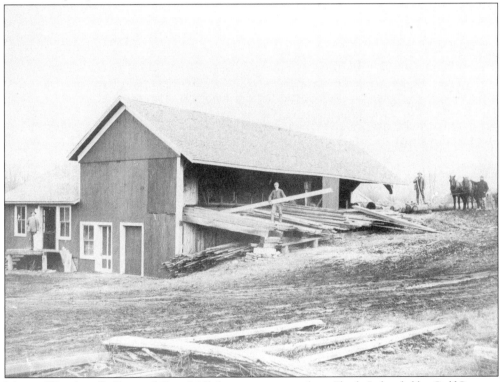

Marcus Woodward's Saw and Grist Mill drew waterpower from Shady Lake, fed by Gulf Stream. The mills were located near the center of town on South Road (shown on the 1869 map). W.C. Pease and William Desso commercially cut ice from the lake.

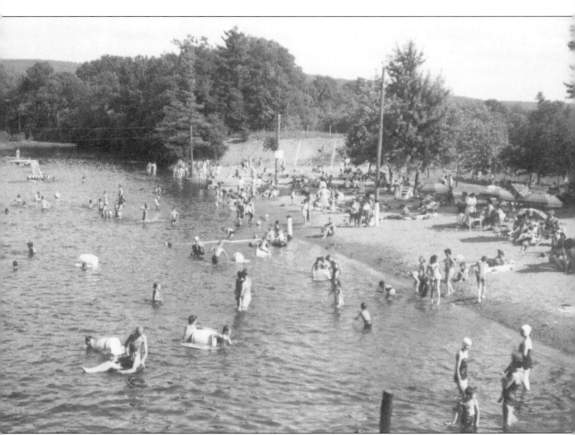

In the 1930s and later, Shady Lake was a popular recreational swimming and picnic area with bathhouses, picnic tables, snack bar, and other buildings. It is owned by the Romanos, who found it necessary to close it down because of the high cost of liability insurance. The pond is still beautiful, but the area is overgrown and the buildings are gone. One hopes the area will find a new use.

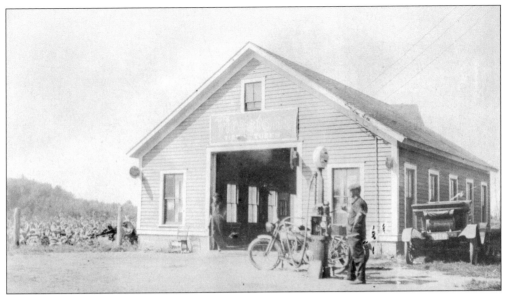

Fred Field's garage, built in 1914, was located at what is now 62 South Road. This 1920 picture shows Fred Field at the pump and his son, Chester Field, by the automobile. The building is now an antiques store.

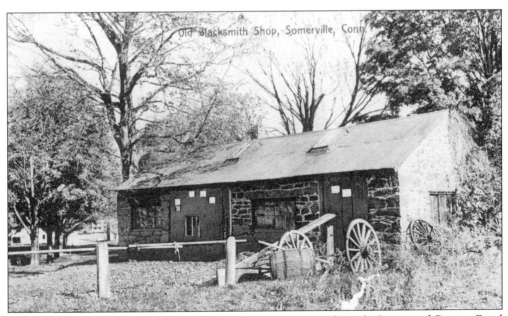

In 1835, Frederick Loomer bought land at the intersection of Maple Street and Pinney Road and built this brownstone blacksmith shop, which he ran until 1860. Later blacksmiths included his son Otis, Henry Rogers, and Lambert Cady. It is now a thrift shop operated by the Somersville Church Ladies Aid.

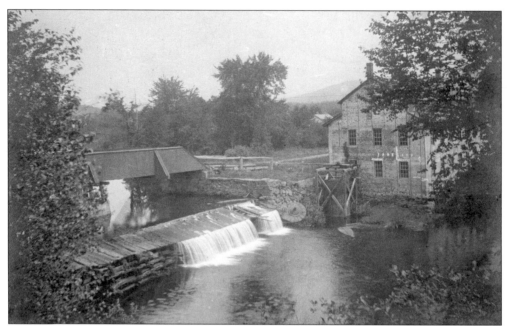

The old Batting Mill was located on Kibbe Grove Road by the Scantic River in North Somers. The building was gone by the 1920s, but the dammed-up pond provided a swimming and picnic area called Kibbe Grove. The dam was washed out in the 1938 hurricane and the pond no longer exists.

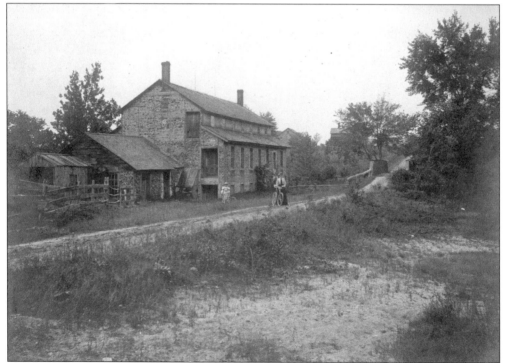

Here, the street side of the old Batting Mill building can be seen. Members of the King or Davis family may have run the mill. There are no signs of anything remaining today.

84

The Mills at Somersville

At about the time Somers was incorporated as a town in the 1730s, Samuel Billings emigrated from England to Enfield and then to Somers. He built a gristmill and a sawmill on the Scantic River in the western part of town. The area was called Billings Mills. He built for himself the house at the intersection of Maple and School Streets, facing the mill. He soon added a fulling mill, and by 1834 there was a brick building beside the large wooden building. In 1835, these mills were bought by Chester Spencer and his nephews, James and William Chaffee. As the Chaffees were more interested in the mercantile business, they left to make fortunes elsewhere, dissolving the partnership. Chester Spencer was a stockholder in the cloth company called the Somersville Company, which ran the mill until it was foreclosed in 1852.

In 1853, Holmes and Reynolds & Company bought the property, enlarged it, and ran the textile mill as well as the gristmill and sawmill for 25 years. The company put up a few workers' houses along School and Main Streets. Rockwell Keeney had worked in this mill earlier in his life and had been running a similar mill in Massachusetts when he married Somers girl Leonora Gowdy and decided to relocate in Somersville with his sons, George, Lafayette, and Mayro. They bought the mills and the surrounding homes for the workers and for their own residences. This became a very profitable venture for them, especially during the two world wars, when their woolen cloth supplied material for blankets and coats for the servicemen. They erected many more workers' homes (especially along Quality Avenue) and imported skilled workmen from abroad, which added a large, predominantly Catholic immigrant population to the village of Somersville. By 1969, when the Environmental Protection Agency (EPA) demanded that process effluents be treated, the Keeneys decided it was more than they could manage with the equipment on hand and they dissolved the business. Since 1969, various operations have been in the buildings, but the textile mill has remained vacant and in litigation for many years.

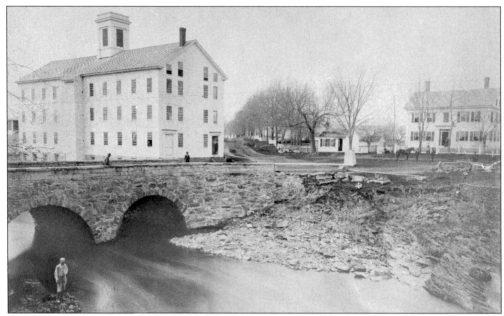

This wooden mill building stands where Samuel Billings had set up business on the Scantic River before the Revolutionary War. It was probably a fulling mill originally. The small building to the right was the mill office, which still stands. Maple Street leads north between the mill and the office. The dam lies beyond the right side of the picture. (Loan, Tim and Mary Keeney.)

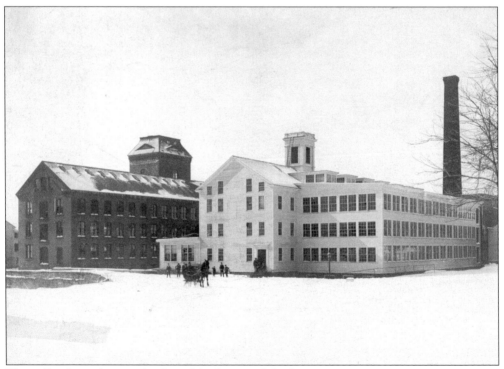

The mill is shown here in the days of the horse and sleigh.

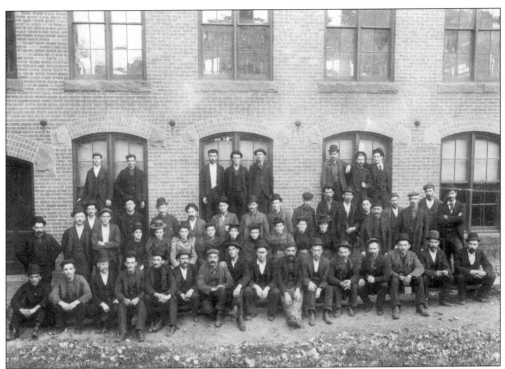

Mill workers pose outside the brick mill building in a picture that probably dates to the early 1920s.

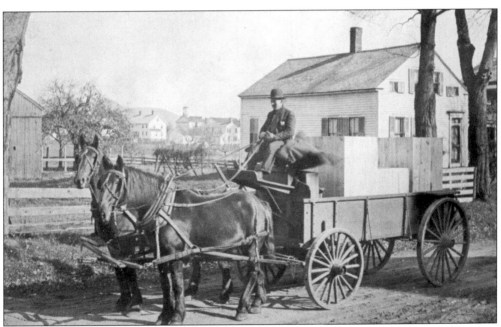

Before 1888, goods were carried from the mill to the railroad by horse and wagon. This man, who spoke little English, was known as "Joe Wagon." He travels north on Maple Street, with School Street and the Spiritualist church in the background.

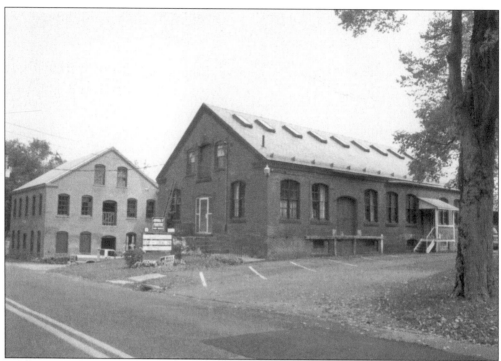

These mill buildings are on the east side of Maple Street. The building on the left was the original sawmill and gristmill; it is now a woodworking shop. The nearer building was a showroom and salesroom that has since been a craft shop and Eastwood Auto Machine, a motor repair shop. (Loan, Tim and Mary Keeney.)

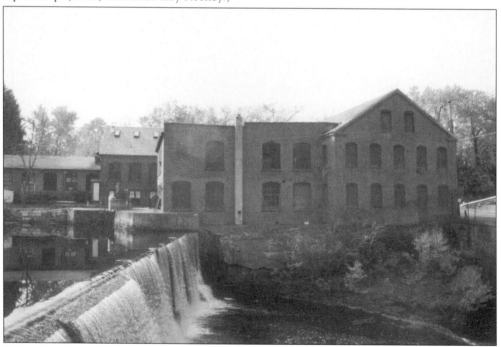

This older picture of the dam and waterfall shows another view of the buildings seen above.

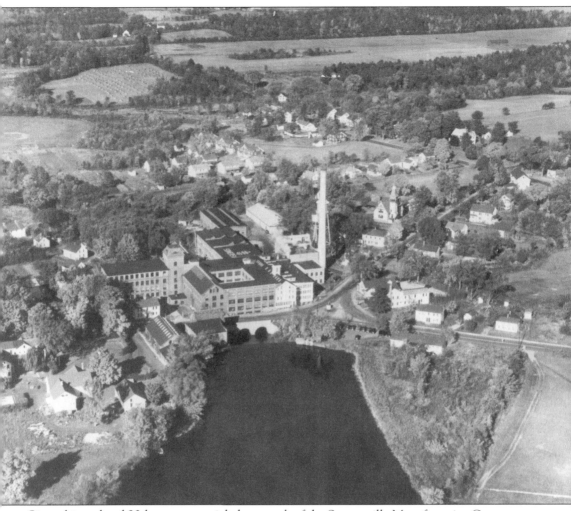

Since this undated 20th-century aerial photograph of the Somersville Manufacturing Company was taken, several structures no longer stand: the old hotel in front of the left wing of the brick mill building, two small houses below the post office building, all the buildings at the far left center, the Keeney swimming pool at the far left near the bottom of the picture, and the smokestack. The millpond and the mill complex are very much in evidence. The top part of the picture gives us a good idea of how much more rural Somersville was only a few years ago. (Loan, Tim and Mary Keeney.)

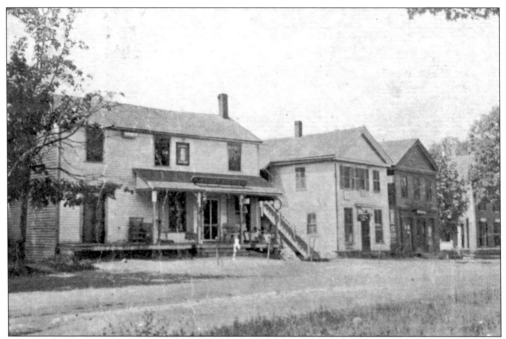

Main Street in Somers is shown *c.* 1920. The buildings along the south side of the street are, from left to right, the Fuller-Bugbee store, two shops that went through a series of uses, and the Woodward House.

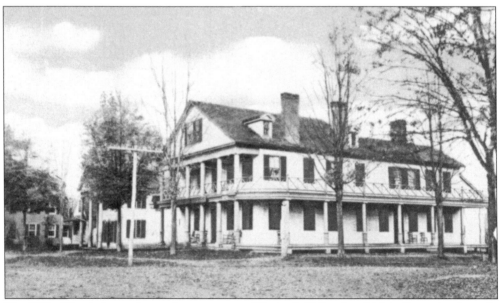

The Kibbe Hotel sits on the northwest corner of Springfield Road and Main Street in the early 1900s. At this time, it was run by Warren Kibbe, who had a large farm along the west side of Springfield Road, north of the hotel. It is now the Somers Inn.

Six
PEOPLE REMEMBERED

Many delightful and interesting people figured importantly in the growth and prosperity of Somers. They are memorialized today in place names, plaques, written histories, and in the fond recollections of present-day Somers residents.

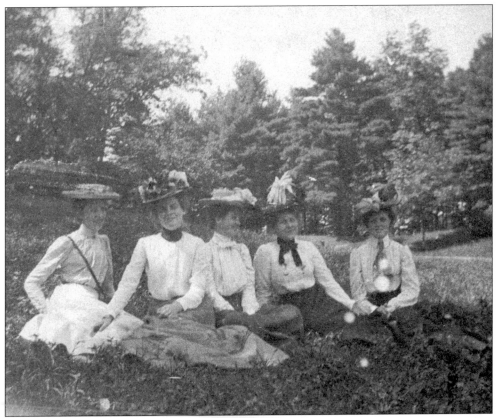

These folks picnic at Forest Park in Springfield in the early 1900s.

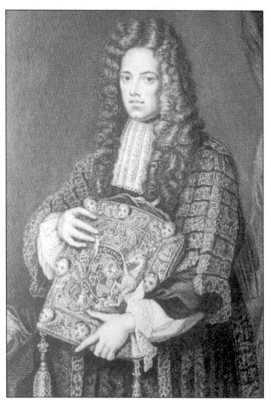

This portrait shows Sir John Somers, lord chancellor of England. The town of Somers was named after Lord Somers in 1734, having been formed as the society of East Enfield c. 1724. Sir John never visited the area and, having died in 1716, was unaware that these colonists had remembered him. Somers, Connecticut, is not to be confused with Somers, New York.

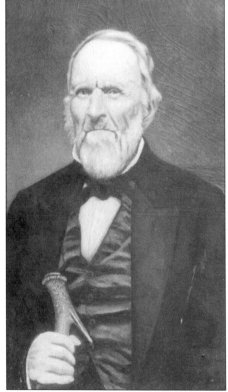

William Collins (1774–1869) built a home at 327 Ninth District Road. One daughter of his large family was Laurinda Collins Whitney, who funded the building of the first public library in Somers in 1896. This portrait, which hangs in the library (now a museum), was painted by Henry Shaw.

Upon his retirement, successful businessman Henry Root Kibbe (1825–1909) built his mansion, Piedmont, in 1883. In the late 1800s, this beautiful home was a social center for the elite of Somers.

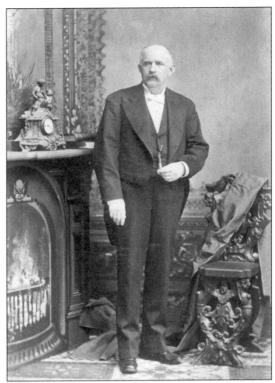

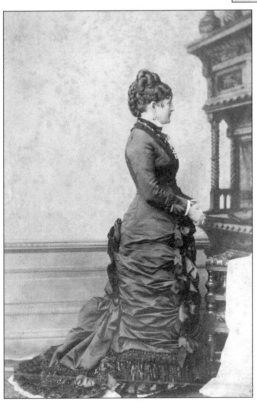

Mabel Gager Kibbe (1835–1923), wife of Henry Root Kibbe, appears here on her silver wedding anniversary.

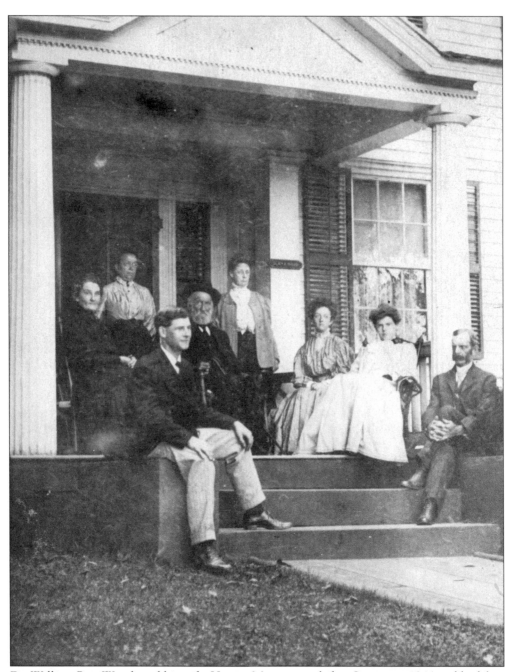

Dr. William Barr Woods and his wife, Harriet Morgan, settled in Somers in 1844 and had four daughters: Mary, Catherine, Harriet, and Alice. He was Somers's revered town doctor through his entire career, save for military service as a surgeon in the Civil War. In this photograph, Dr. Woods sits behind his grandson Charles W.W. Pease amid friends and family at the house at 653 Main Street. The house was sold in the 1950s by Dr. Woods's great-granddaughter Helen Pease Starbuck and is now Donald Kennett's residence.

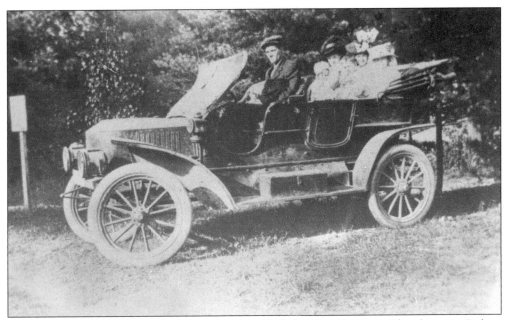

The Galbraith family is ready for a ride in a 1908 Stanley Steamer. The driver is Robert Galbraith. Accompanying him are Florence Aborn Galbraith, Elmira A. Galbraith, Ruth Prior, and children, and Florence and Robert Galbraith.

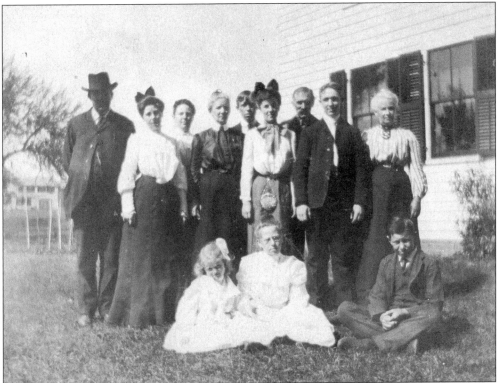

The Worthington family is gathered in this picture. Penciled notations attest that Aunt Annie, Uncle Charlie, and Hazel are in the group.

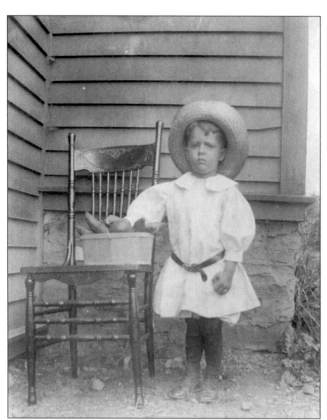

George Van Kleeck is about two-and-a-half years old in this *c.* 1900 photograph.

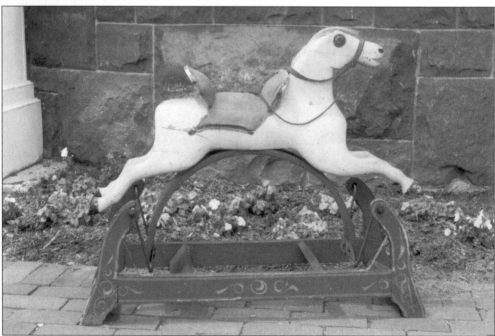

This rocking horse, which is now on display at the Somers Historical Museum, belonged to George Van Kleeck.

Judge Charles S. Fuller (probate judge, 1859–1922) was the son of Judge Solomon Fuller. Charles was influential in the decision of Laurinda Collins Whitney to donate the Somers Free Public Library in 1896. Judge Fuller was also co-chairman with Julia Chism Gowdy of Somers's bicentennial celebration in 1934.

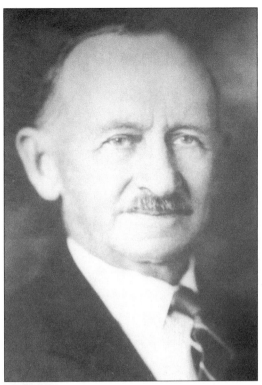

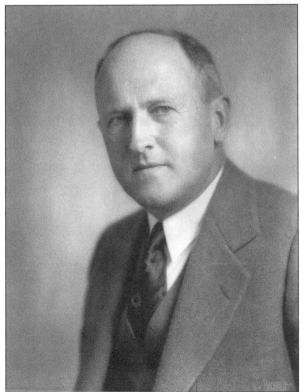

Judge Ernest S. Fuller (1879–1945) was the third in his family to serve as a probate judge. He lived in the Piedmont mansion and was very active in the social and political life of the community. In 1929, Judge Fuller and his wife, Mabel Kibbe Fuller, donated the first modern public school, the Kibbe-Fuller School, to the Town of Somers.

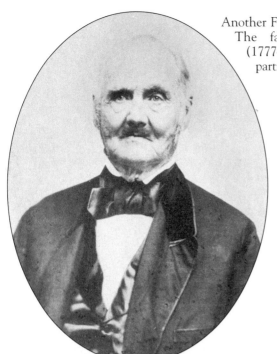

Another Fuller family had an impact on the town. The family included Capt. Isaac Fuller (1777–1845), grandfather of Willard Fuller and partner in the Fuller-Bugbee store.

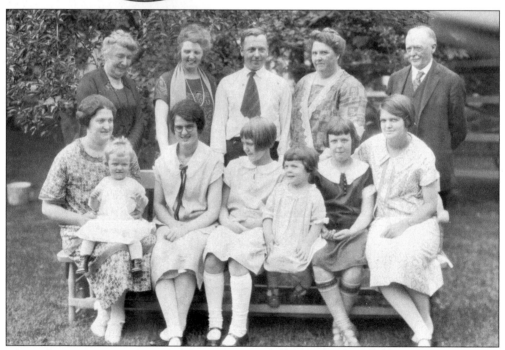

The Fuller-Bugbee family appears here in 1927. They ran grocery stores in Somersville and Somers until the 1930s. Seated with the children are the adult Bugbee daughters, from left to right, as follows: Marguerite Bugbee Bliss (1901–1982), Isabelle Bugbee Howes (1904–1992), and Emily Bugbee (1902–1999). Standing fourth from the left is their mother, Etta Fuller Bugbee (1877–1958). Their grandfather, Willard Fuller (1850–1931), stands on the far right.

Two Somers Zoning Commission members, A. Vail Smith Jr., judge of probate (seated), and Horace Pease Jr. are at work. Horace was one of the first to participate in the Connecticut Farmland Preservation Act in 1983. Other Somers farms in the program were the Pinney and LaChance-Moser farms.

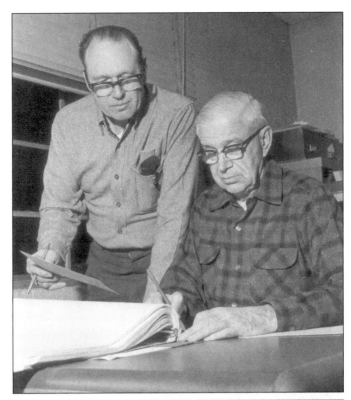

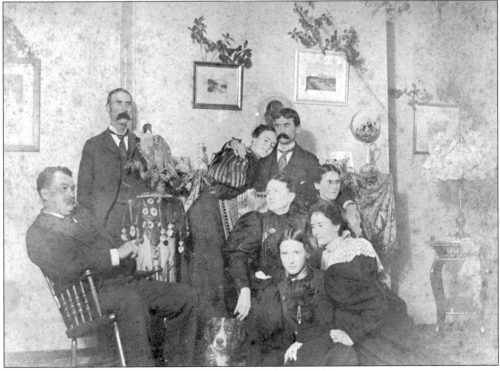

The Horace Pease Sr. family poses for a picture in the Gay Nineties.

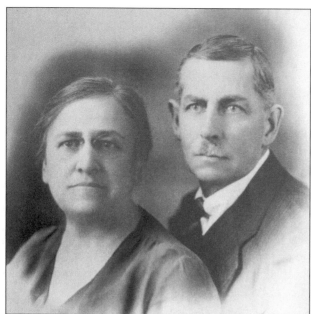

Louis A. Gowdy (1872–1972) and his second wife, Julia Chism Gowdy, were pillars of the Somersville Congregational Church. Louis was a successful farmer who raised tobacco and provided milk for the Somers Creamery. He was a representative from Somers in the Connecticut legislature and held many offices in town.

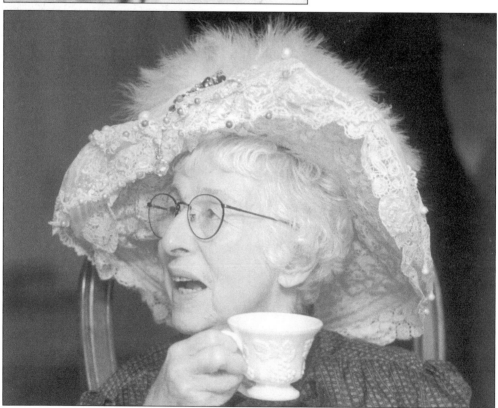

Olive Louise Chism (1919–1998), well-loved teacher, school principal, author, and poet is shown at a fundraiser tea party. She was raised in Somers at the Gowdy farm by her father's sister, Julia Chism Gowdy, after her mother succumbed to influenza shortly after her birth. This striking image was recorded by Sherry Peters of the *Hartford Courant*.

The Louis Boucher family came with the Keeneys to Somersville in 1879. Louis, formerly from Canada, was a wheelwright. He had a son, Charles, and five daughters, Clara Webb, Louise Robbins, Lizzie Traverse, Rose Hebert, and Mary Bourque.

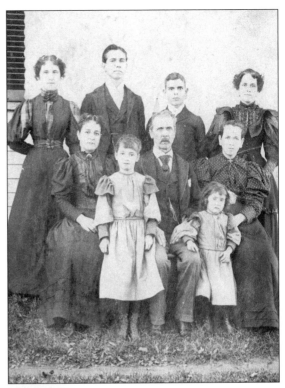

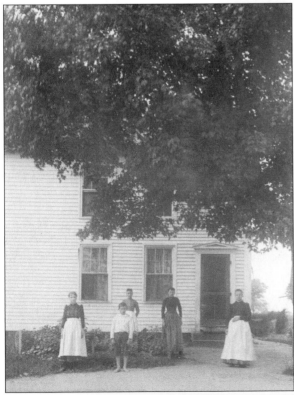

The Bourque family poses for the Howes Brothers photographers outside their home (the long-block workers home) on School Street in Somersville.

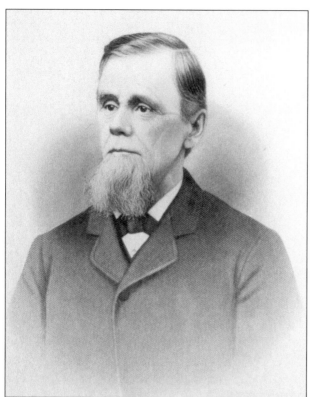

Rockwell Keeney (1822–1901) was born in Manchester, Connecticut; he and his sons, Lafayette and George, founded the Somersville Manufacturing Company in 1879. He was married to Leonora Gowdy and they had seven children. The mill was very successful during both world wars. Even in business concerns, Rockwell was active in community affairs.

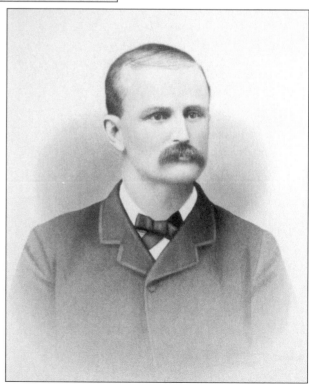

Gen. George E. Keeney (1849–1923), son of Rockwell, was treasurer and later president of the Somersville Manufacturing Company. He was instrumental in the enlargement and growth of the former satinet mill.

Robert Leland Keeney Sr., son of Lafayette, became treasurer of the Somersville Manufacturing Company. He was active in World War I in the foreign service of the Red Cross, being most notably in charge of relief efforts in Italy after the Austrian retreat. He married Harriet Elwood and they had six children, including the youngest John (Jack) Henry, who is still living; the late Harriet Pinney; William; Robert Jr.; Raymond, who lost his life in a World War II plane crash; and Elise Irving.

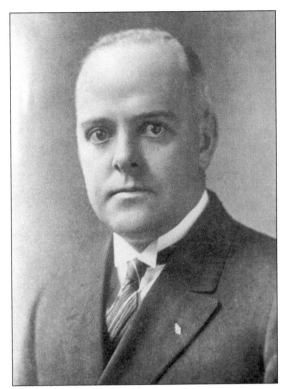

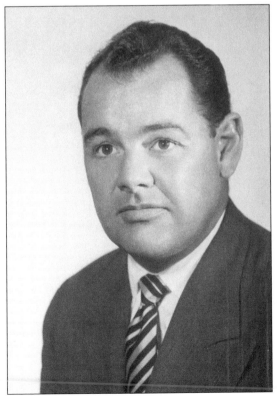

Robert L. (Bob) Keeney Jr. (1919–1985), an heir to the Somersville Manufacturing Company, was active in the business until it closed in 1968. He was also active in civic affairs and served on boards of banks, hospitals, and with his own business in plastic and industrial films. He served four terms in the Connecticut House of Representatives in Hartford. He and his wife, Jane Todhunter, had six sons and a daughter.

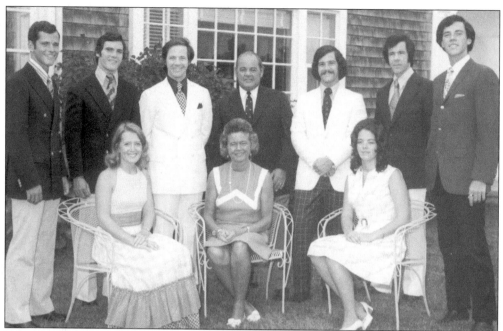

Taken in 1972, this portrait shows the Bob Keeney family, from left to right, as follows: (sitting) Miss Jane, mother Jane, and Janey; (standing) Timothy, Jamie, Robert III, father Robert Jr., Denison, Raymond, and Todhunter.

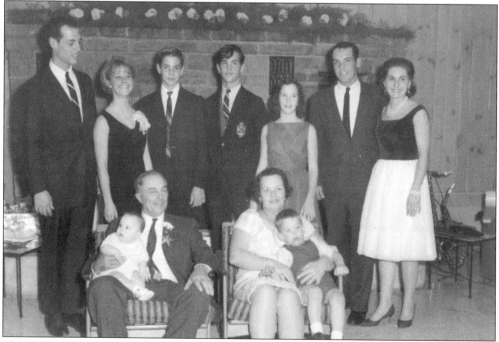

The Willard Pinney family had this picture taken in 1965. Sitting in the front are Willard and his wife, Harriet Keeney Pinney. They are holding Leland's sons, Leland (Gus) and Sampson. Standing in the back are, from left to right, Willard Jr., Christine, David, John, Harriet (Tia), Leland, and Sally (Leland's wife).

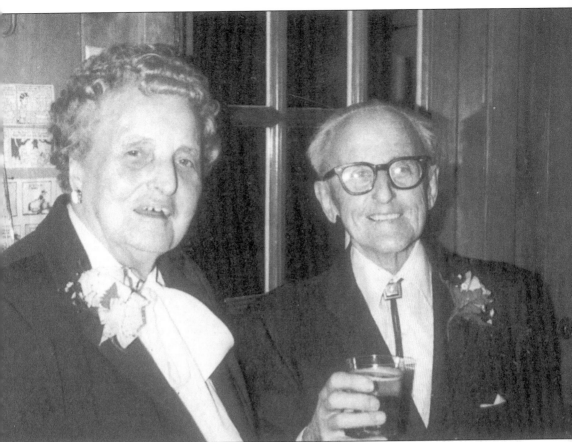

George Schiessl was the gracious maitre d' of the Somers Inn from 1938 to 1966 in association with his wife, Emmy (Joerg) Schiessl, and Alphons and Hilda (Schiessl) Joerg. He was endlessly cheerful and thoughtful; on any given day at 2:00 p.m. sharp, he could be seen taking lunch to Mrs. Pio at her variety shop across the street. George was a talented musician, serving as organist and soloist for All Saints Church and performing frequently with the Village Players. While he was honored by the Rotary and Lions clubs among others, he is perhaps best remembered by succeeding generations of children as a sprightly and beloved school crossing guard. In 1996, at age 98, he was an enthusiastic onlooker at the relocation of the old Free Public Library.

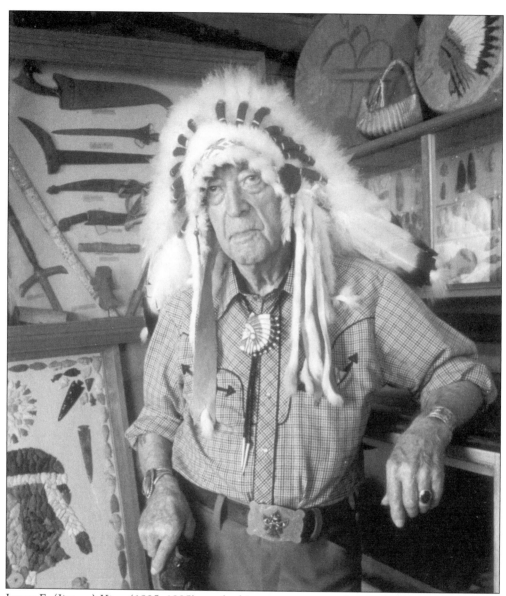

James F. (Jimmy) King (1895–1985) was by his own account a showman who traveled with a troupe of Native Americans led by Chief Red Cloud, providing authenticity and balance to the presentations of better-known figures like Bill Cody. He undoubtedly led a colorful life to the point that common sense questions the line between logic and legend. He first began gathering Americana while serving as a manager of the East Indian League. In 1950, he built a museum to display his collection; still bristling at being "shushed" in a Worcester museum as a child, he ran the museum admission-free until his death in 1985. He was featured in a 1984 article in *Yankee* magazine. He retailed turquoise jewelry and souvenirs to support himself and his wife, Lenore. Alan Bicknell, once curator of the museum, says that King reported seeing eagles, children of the Great Spirit, flying over the museum. Bicknell felt that unlikely, given King's failing eyesight, but within a month after King's death, Bicknell himself saw two eagles. (Loan, Michael Stenz, current owner of Somers Mountain Museum.)

Seven

ORGANIZATIONS
AND EVENTS

Somers, a community of energetic people in a small country town just outside convenient everyday access to Springfield or Hartford, had to devise its own homegrown entertainment. Church groups, civic clubs, and volunteer activities provided useful leisure occupation suited to every taste.

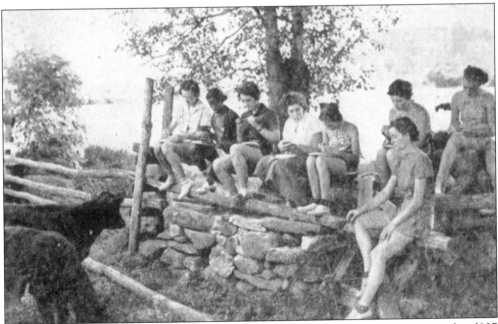

Camp Aya-Po (from a Native American phrase meaning "carry it on") was organized in 1927 by the YWCA of Hartford. It was developed on an existing pond, now Lake Aya-Po, off Camp Road. The camp is active all summer long. Here, a troop of campers pauses during a woodsy ramble. The Village Players present their fall dinner-theater plays in the camp's dining hall.

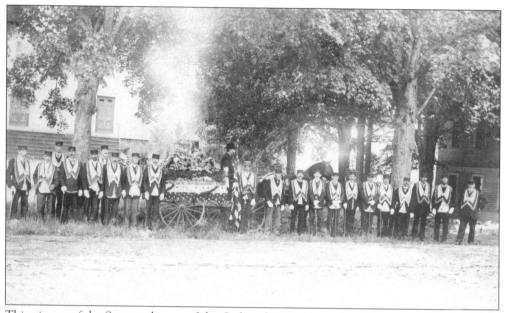

This picture of the Somers chapter of the Order of United American Mechanics (OUAM) was taken in front of Piedmont Hall with a float for the Four Town Fair parade. The OUAM was ultrapatriotic, advocating a flag in every classroom, morning prayers in school, and restriction of immigration. The OUAM was established after the Civil War and disbanded shortly after World War I.

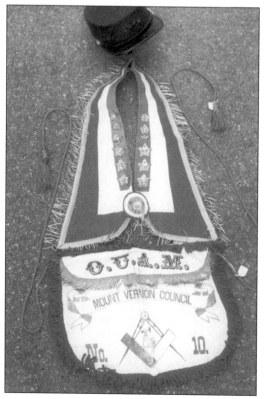

This OAUM regalia, worn by Edwin Theodore Hurlburt, is very colorful in red, white, and blue with a navy visored cap, an elaborate collar, and an apron similar to that worn by the Masons.

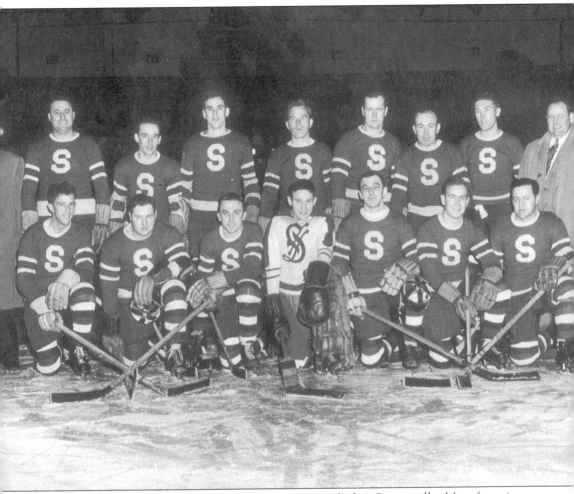

The Somersville Hockey Club champions represented the Somersville Manufacturing Company in the Industrial League, playing to large crowds of loyal fans against the Bigelow-Sanford Mill and the Springfield teams. They practiced on local pond ice from November to March and were so good that opposing teams accused the Somersville Manufacturing Company of "packing the roster" with Canadians. The team included the following members: (left wing) N. Cormier, J.W. Rackis, F. Buvarsky, and R. Cormier; (right wing) E. Ramsey, C. Kareski, J.J. Rackis, and A. Mikulski; (left defense) R. Bourque and A. Grigitis; (right defense) W. Balsewicz and J. Butkus.

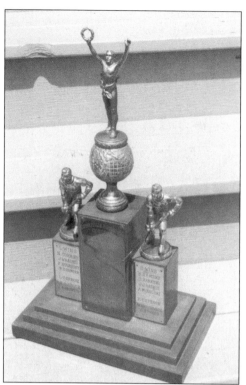

The Somersville Hockey Club won this Industrial League championship trophy in 1941–1942. The team included goalie R. Ramsey, center A. Kozikowski, C. Padegimas, A. Cormier, T. Strekas, E. Burgess, manager J. Butkus, coach B. Underwood, assistant coach F. Gould, and trainer L. Cormier. (Donation, Cathy Butkus.)

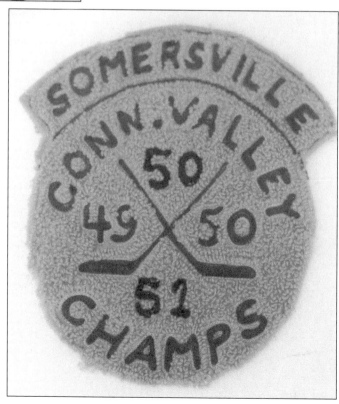

Edward Burgess donated this hockey sweater patch.

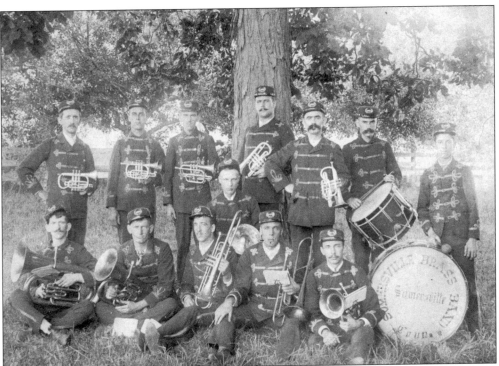

The Somersville mill band, as pictured in this 1891 Howes Brothers photograph, was made up of workers at the Somersville Manufacturing Company. Seated in the center is Peter Halpin, a spinner by trade. His grandson Robert "Buddy" Halpin of Somers carries on his grandfather's musical tradition as a member of Memories, a big band orchestra.

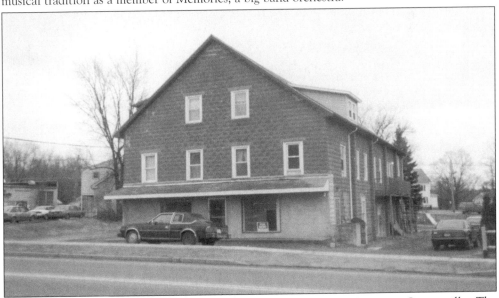

The Foresters of America built this meeting hall at 156 Main Street in Somersville. The Canadian Catholic fraternal organization provided death insurance and care for members' families. Foresters Hall has been used for dances, dinners, moving pictures, and prizefights. Today, it is a storefront with apartments upstairs.

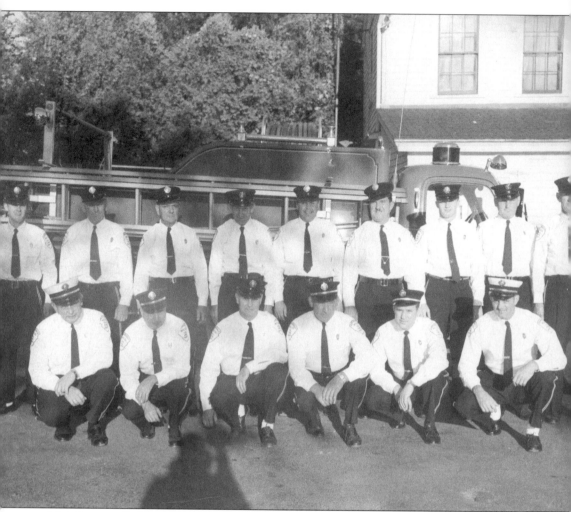

The Somersville Manufacturing Company Fire Department appears in this 1950s image. The members are, from left to right, as follows: (front row) Deputy Chief Lennie Lakonski, Ed Bourgoise, Ellsworth Wood, Tony Padegimas, John Kozikowski, and Chief Lloyd Hunt; (back row) Joe Grigas, Pete Unas, Alphonse Bouthiette, Custy Labutis, Bill Taylor, Ray Burgess, unidentified, Ben Paterwic, and Egan Murawski. Organized to protect the mill and associated residences, the department was merged into the Somers Volunteer Fire Department when the mill closed in 1969. (Photograph by Longin Sonski, on loan from Marybeth Sonski Marquardt.)

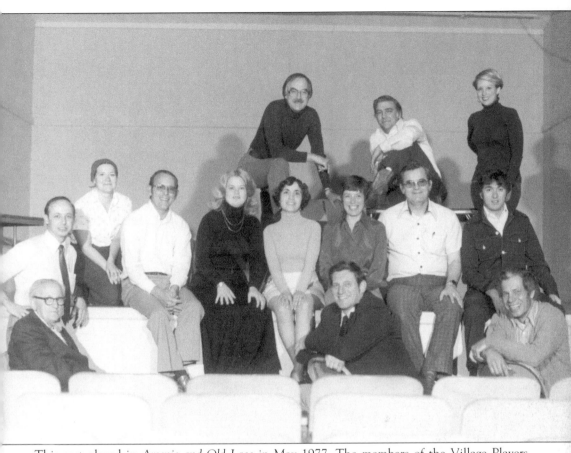

This cast played in *Arsenic and Old Lace* in May 1977. The members of the Village Players include, from left to right, the following: (bottom row) George Schiessl, Ewart Lockyer, and Bob Smith; (middle row) Jim Rogers, Wendy Peterson, Gene Allard, Patti Powers, Sandy Rogers, Jan Stephens, Bill Klase, and Ron Thomas; (top row) Malcolm Chadbourne, Herb Legg, and Suzanne McConnell. Organized in 1971, the group still produces plays. (Donation, Richard Jackson.)

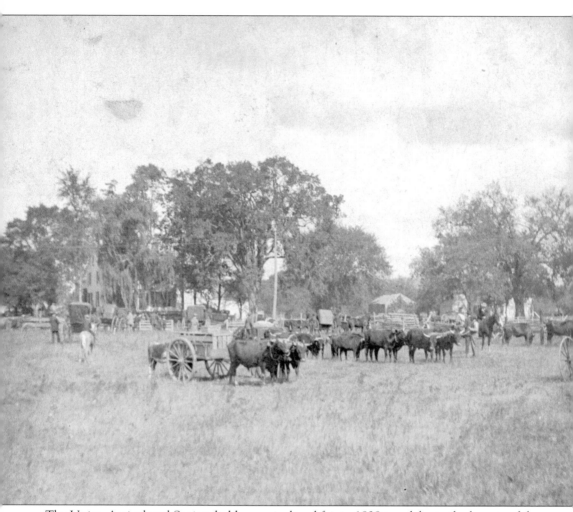

The Union Agricultural Society held an agricultural fair in 1838 to celebrate the bounty of the towns of East Windsor, Ellington, Enfield, and Somers. Its first gathering was in Somers, but each of the four towns hosted the event in sequence—hence, the Four Town Fair. The chosen site was typically near the center of the village. This scene occurred in the field now urbanized as Kibbe Drive. In Somers, other exhibits were shown in the church basement, and food was provided by local groups, with dancing at Mechanics Hall.

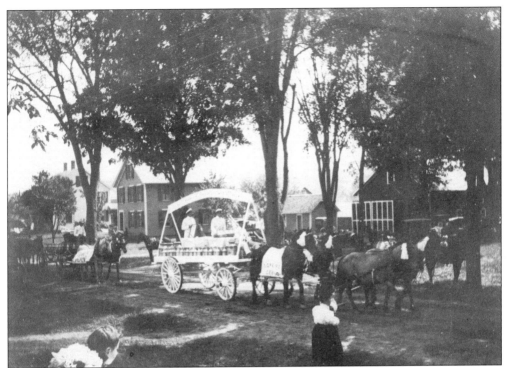

This float appeared in the Four Town Fair parade in the early 1900s. The parade is still an annual event and follows a route from the center of Somers to the Egypt Road fairground. (Loan, K. Welch.)

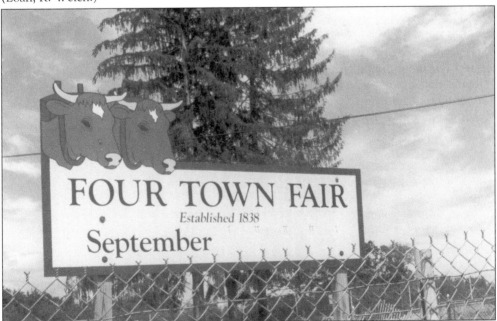

In 1960, the Union Agricultural Society purchased permanent grounds for the Four Town Fair on Egypt Road. The spacious area, with exhibit buildings and other facilities, is used for town events, 4-H fairs, and is rented for large-group gatherings.

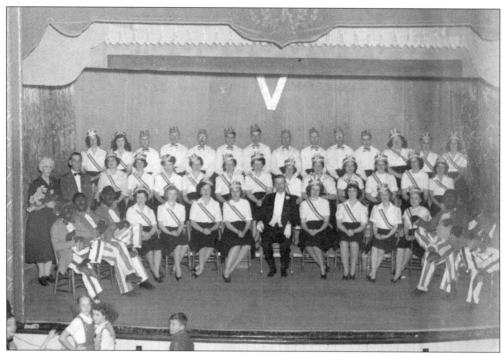

This minstrel show was performed in the 1940s as a patriotic fundraiser for the war effort. Notice the V for "victory." (Loan K. Welch.)

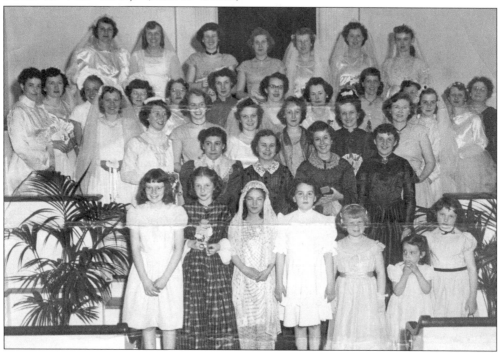

The Somers Junior Women's Club presented this March of Brides show in 1950, modeling original authentic bridal gowns from 1839 to 1949. (Loan, K. Welch, who appears in the second row, center.)

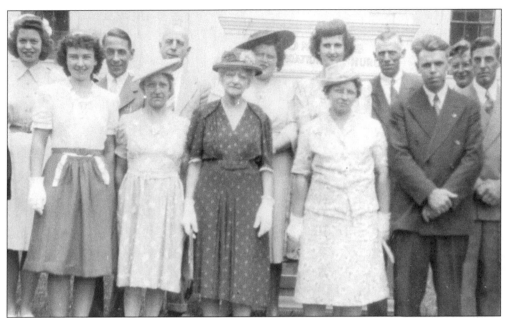

The Grange (Patrons of Husbandry) is a national organization for rural farm families, providing education and social activities. The Somers Grange was always well represented with impressive exhibits and floats in the Four Town Fair. It was organized in 1889 and maintained a building for a time. It later met in the social room of the Somersville Congregational Church until it disbanded in 1998 for lack of farming families. This picture of members from 1940 to 1945 after Grange Sunday services shows, from right to left, the following: (front row) Mary Fitzgerald, Priscilla Avery, Nellie Robbins, Ann Griswold, and Harold Pease Sr.; (back row) Margaret P. Sonski, Fred Mathews, Paul Patenaude, Florence Galbraith, Lucille Kibbe Gordon, John Griswold, Elroy David, and Norman Kibbe. (Donation, M. Sonski.)

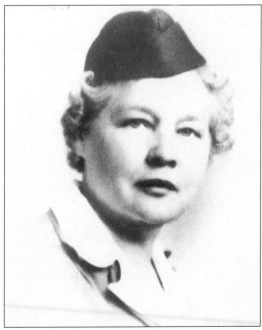

Mary Barkal, R.N., was Somers's first visiting nurse from 1950 to 1965. She worked with Dr. Ralph Thayer until his death in 1960, giving home healthcare advice and organizing well-child clinics. She was able to communicate in Lithuanian and was therefore able to establish trust with the town's immigrants. The Visiting Nurses Association (VNA) continues to aid Somers residents.

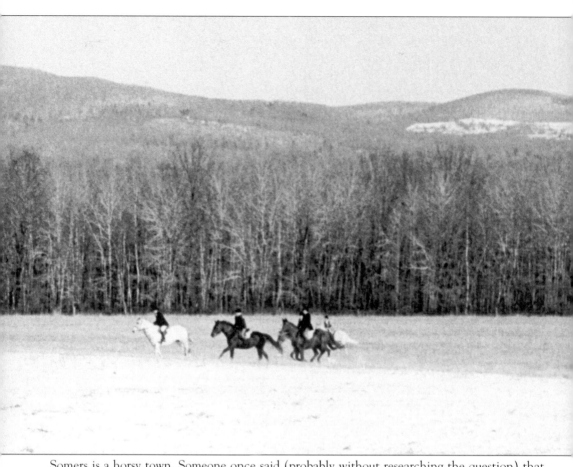

Somers is a horsy town. Someone once said (probably without researching the question) that there are more horses than people in town. Richard Jackson took this 1965 picture of a fox hunt off Hall Hill Road in the area of Carriage Drive. The Reddington Rock Riders hold many equestrian events, and Shallowbrook Stables is internationally known for its polo games. Lindy Farms raises world-class harness racing horses.

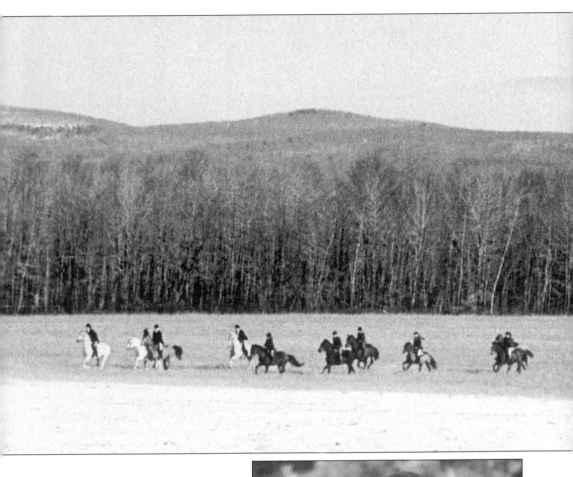

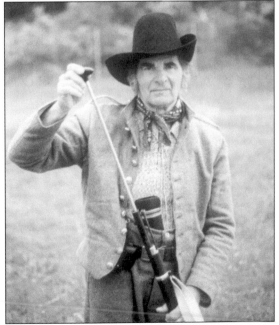

Bill Jones, former president of the Somers Historical Society, participates in the Civil War reenactment on Memorial Day weekend in 1984 at the Four Town Fair fairgrounds. A yearlong celebration of Somers's 250th anniversary preceded this event.

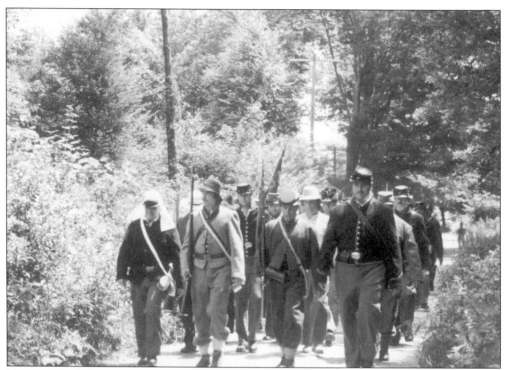

Units of Civil War reenactors descended on Somers from as far as South Carolina to hold an authentic encampment. Here, a mix of Blue and Grey soldiers returns to camp from a mock battle.

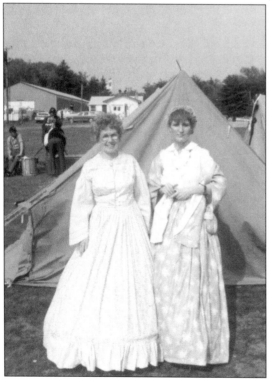

Jeanne and Sara DeBell are shown wearing hoop-skirted costumes that they made for the 250th anniversary of Somers. The whole town was enthusiastically involved, but particular thanks are due to Jeanne (chairman of the celebration); Bill and Mabel Jones of the historical society; Janice Steinmetz of the Union Agricultural Society; and Richard Wright, commander of the third Louisiana regiment, manned by residents of East Longmeadow, Massachusetts. (Loan, Jeanne DeBell.)

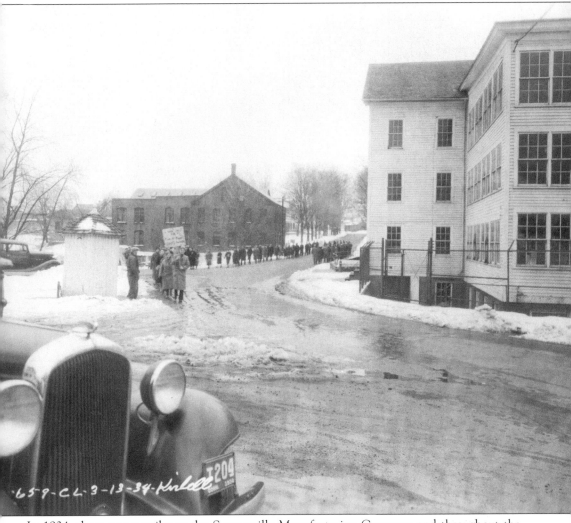

In 1934, there was a strike at the Somersville Manufacturing Company and throughout the state for higher wages for textile workers. The strike lasted three weeks. This view of the picket line looks south on Maple Street.

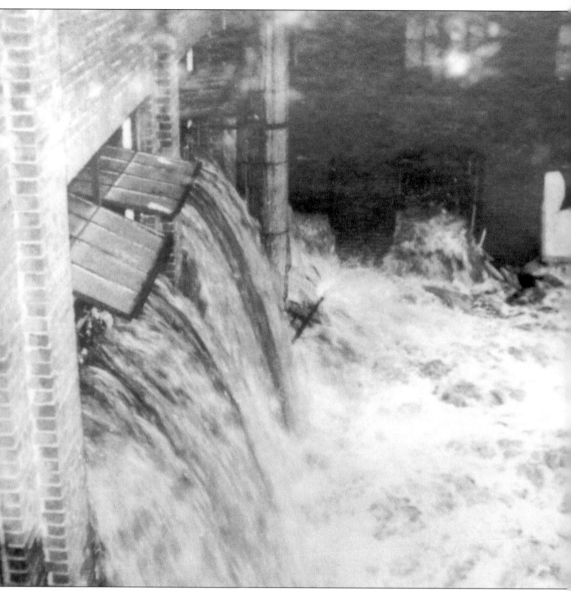

The flood of 1955 occurred after two hurricanes dropped heavy rains in Massachusetts and Connecticut. The Scantic River overflowed the pond and dam, flooding the first floor of the mill. Much machinery and cloth was damaged. The smallest streams swelled into raging rivers that washed out roads, bridges, and buildings. Full recovery took several years.

A Moving Experience

The Somers Historical Society, organized in 1962, used the inactive Somers Free Public Library as a meeting place and a museum. The building was donated to the town by Laurinda Collins Whitney, daughter of William Collins of Somers, who had married James Scollay Whitney, a general and commandant of the Springfield Armory.

This structure, which is listed in the National Register of Historic Places, has stylistically been designated as eclectic. Indeed, its architecture defies classification, blending Colonial Revival, Queen Anne, Georgian, and Greek Revival styles into a very unique and attractive building. Perhaps the most striking features of the building are the recently restored leaded-glass blind arch windows that portray a golden lamp superimposed over a globe. Accompanying these leaded panels on the front façade is an equally striking bow window; each of its three sash windows has 16 bull's-eye panes over a single curved pane.

The town maintained the building for many years, but it had limited use, lacking sidewalks and parking space. Over time the building deteriorated badly. In its 100th year, First Selectman Robert Percoski suggested that if it were moved to town property where it would be more accessible to the public, there might be support for its restoration. A committee of the society—Chuck Alfano, Dan Roulier, and Ralph Lumb—suggested that if the town would fund the move, the society would obligate itself to restore the building at no cost to the town. Thus, in September 1996, the building was moved from its location at 547 Main Street to a lot at 11 Battle Street.

After the move to the site between the Kibbe-Fuller School playground and the senior center, it took two years of hard work by volunteers as well as funds and materials donated by businesses and citizens before the restored building was rededicated in September 1998. As part of the restoration project, a park was created around the building, including an amphitheater. The site is now called Somers Common and the building is the Somers Historical Museum. The Cultural Commission holds summer concerts in the Earl Jahn Amphitheater, and the museum houses rotating displays of Somers artifacts and historical information. A computer-based genealogical center will soon be up and running.

The following photographs illustrate the move of the building and some aspects of its restoration. They are a fine tribute to the townspeople who made it possible to preserve this architecturally unique structure.

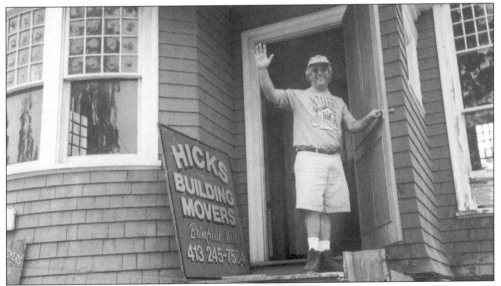

Dan Roulier was one of the prime movers in the preservation of the old library building.

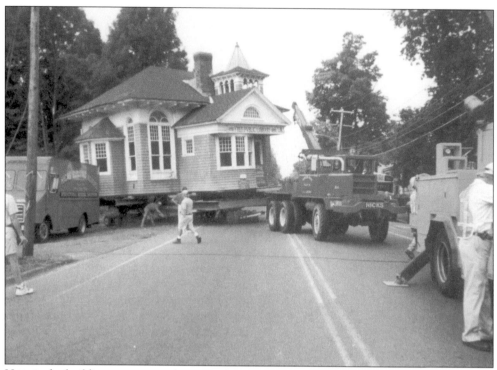

Here is the building as it proceeds east on Main Street.

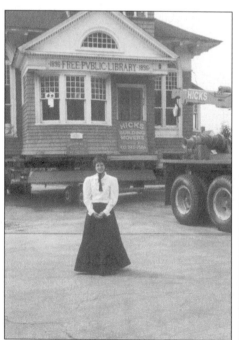

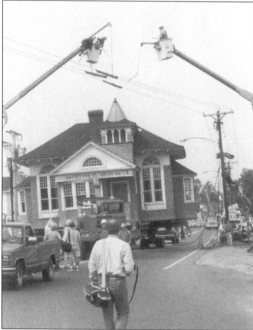

Left: Mary Harrington, president of the Somers Historical Society poses in costume as the building rolls majestically by. *Right:* All the electric, telephone, and traffic signal wires had to be raised to make room for the building to pass.

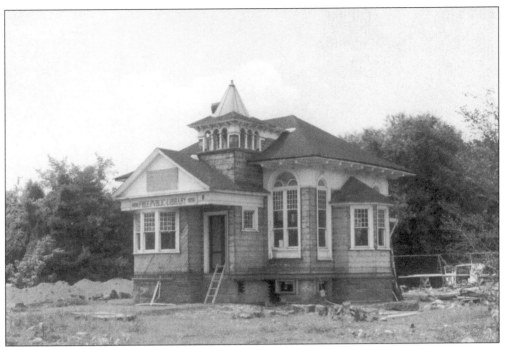

The building has a new foundation and is about to be reshingled.

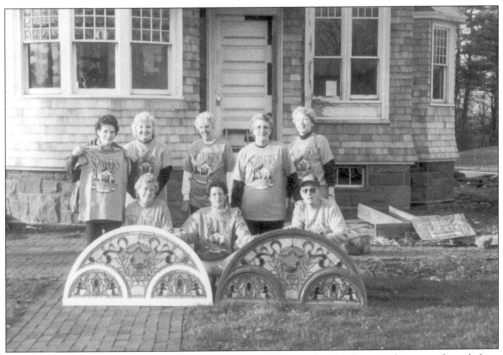

This committee restored the century-old stained-glass windows. The members are, from left to right, as follows: (front row) Shannon Mason, Mary Harrington (president), and Robert Badura; (back row) Jean Heilman, Joanne Chadbourne, Joyce Benson, Tootsie Badura, and Carole Pyne. (Loan, Carole Pyne.)

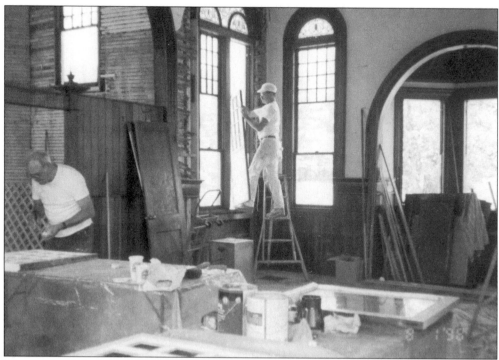

The inside of the building is under restoration by Ralph Lumb, who is painting a window as master painter Mike Eldridge hangs a window.

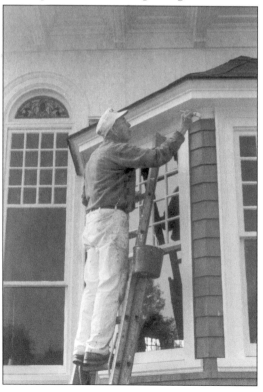

Don Stevenson paints some of the trim.

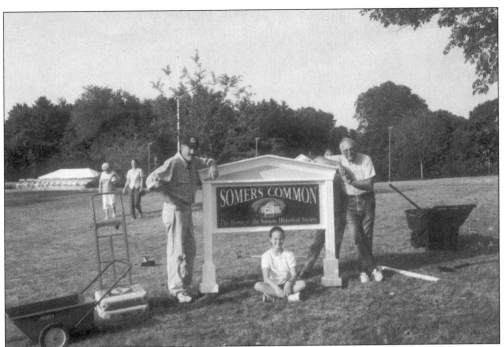

Chuck Alfano, chairman of the restoration committee, and his daughter Caitlin help Ralph Lumb erect the sign on Somers Common, created as the site for the restored building.

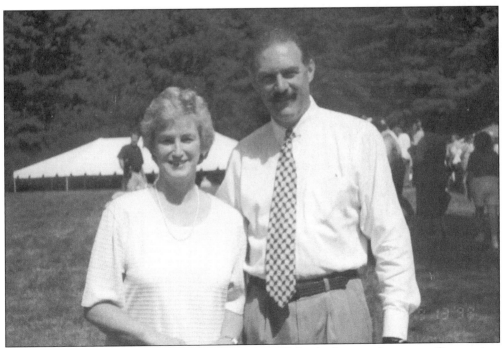

In September 1998, a rededication ceremony was held for the historical museum. Connecticut Lt. Gov. Jodi Rell and Chuck Alfano were among those who spoke.

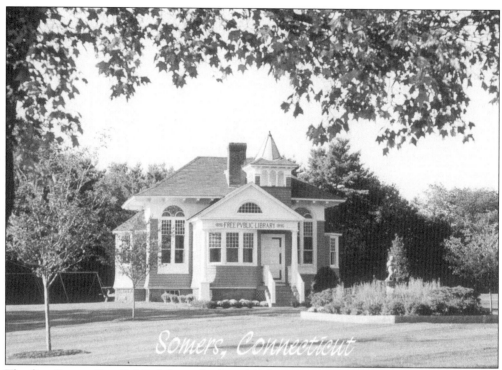

The first Somers Free Public Library, built in 1896, was moved to 11 Battle Street in 1996. It was restored and rededicated as the Somers Historical Museum in 1998.

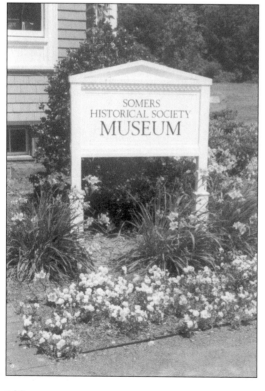

Shown is the sign for the new museum.